WHAT PEOPLE ARE SAYING ABOUT

THE DRUID SHAMAN

A sound, practical introduction to a com~ ~ide-ranging subject. Danu Forest's guidance chi~ my own experience of working with spir~ ~grating folk traditions, literary so~ ~ contemporary practice, Danu c ~nd spiritually apposite ideas with sens ~ning our relations with spirit, as well as work. ~ed sites. As Danu says, how we perceive the spirits we ~ect with as Druids does make a difference.

Having been plugging the notion of Druidry as the native 'shamanic' tradition of Britain and Europe since 1974, it's good to see that it's increasingly catching on, not only amongst fellow Druids, but also amongst archaeologists. I believe we are heading in a direction that links us very firmly with the spirit of ancient Druidry. This is what I call rekindling the sacred fire of Druidry, and I believe Danu Forest's 'The Druid Shaman' will play a part in this rekindling.

Philip Shallcrass -'Greywolf' Chief of the British Druid Order.

Another slim volume. Can't be much in that, you might think. And if you do, you would think wrong. This is an introduction to a complex subject and to write a primer with such clarity as this author has done requires a deep understanding of the subject and an equally deep understanding of how to communicate that to others. I particularly enjoyed the emphasis in this book on balance, on personal responsibility, and on service.

That is why this book introduces you to the basics and no more. You have to make the journey; you have to establish a relationship with the worlds beyond and those who live there. No one else can do that for you and there is no system beyond what you will learn here. You can read more deeply into the subject if you wish, but that won't make the journey any easier. There are no secrets beyond the one revealed in this book... It is your journey and your relationship. You can only learn more about that by doing it, by journeying as often as you can.

Clear and unpretentious, based on good and thorough research as well as sensible practice, and full of sound advice; you really do not need any other introduction to this subject.

Greame Talboys

The Druid Shaman

Exploring the Celtic Otherworld

SHAMAN PATHWAYS

The Druid Shaman

Exploring the Celtic Otherworld

Danu Forest

MOON
BOOKS

Winchester, UK
Washington, USA

First published by Moon Books, 2013
Moon Books is an imprint of John Hunt Publishing Ltd., Laurel House, Station Approach,
Alresford, Hants, SO24 9JH, UK
office1@jhpbooks.net
www.johnhuntpublishing.com
www.moon-books.net

For distributor details and how to order please visit the 'Ordering' section on our website.

Text copyright: Danu Forest 2013

ISBN: 978 1 78099 615 8

A CIP catalogue record for this book is available from the British Library.

Design: Stuart Davies
www.stuartdaviesart.com

Printed and bound by CPI Group (UK) Ltd, Croydon, CR0 4YY

We operate a distinctive and ethical publishing philosophy in all
areas of our business, from our global network of authors to
production and worldwide distribution.

CONTENTS

Introduction

I have been in a multitude of shapes,
Before I assumed a consistent form.
I have been a sword, narrow, variegated...
I have been a tear in the air,
I have been the dullest of stars.
I have been a word among letters,
I have been a book in the origin.
I have been the light of lanterns...
I have been a course, I have been an eagle.
I have been a coracle in the seas:
I have been compliant in the banquet.
I have been a drop in a shower;
Taliesin, *Cad Goddeu*[1]

These words, recorded in the 14th century as earlier works by the 6th-century shaman bard Taliesin, vividly convey a profound experience of communion with what could be called today the 'world soul' or *Anima Mundi*. This state of connection between the individual and the sum of all things or beings upon the earth is a deeply shamanic state of consciousness, transcending the constraints of the body and entering into an expanded awareness, encompassing an infinite number of points of view simultaneously. Here the visionary qualities and potential of the Celtic bardic tradition result in the poet or bard drawing in the gift of divine inspiration from the spirit world, experiencing this expanded ecstatic awareness, and attaining the knowledge or wisdom of the gods.

The *Cad Goddeu*, or 'battle of the trees', is an intriguing poem about a conflict between the mortal world and the Welsh Otherworld, Annwn. Here we encounter the liminal point where both worlds meet seen through the eyes of the magician

Gwydion, on one layer, and through the bardic medium of Taliesin, on another. In its lines we encounter world upon world, experience upon experience, layered and compacted upon one another, connecting, challenging, locked in exchange and inter-change. This is the realm of the Celtic, or druid shaman; meeting the Otherworld and the realms of spirit, yet firmly placed in the traditions and knowledge of our Celtic-Irish and British ancestral lore, allied with the trees and the spirits of these green isles, and drawing upon a wellspring of indigenous wisdom going back millennia.

While a great deal has been lost over the last two thousand years, it is still possible to track our way along the old roads, and retrace our ancestral footsteps into a relationship with spirit that is still vividly and passionately Celtic, and druidic in nature. In this book, we shall be exploring the realm of the druid shaman, primarily through experience and practice. Drawing from the deep roots of Celtic druidry, and its surviving literature, we shall seek divine inspiration for ourselves, and discover our own ways of working, drawn from their knowledge. The path ahead relies on our common sense, and an intuitive gift for feeling the way, peeling back layers of meaning, and boldly exploring the realms of spirit, aided by allies that walked these roads with our kin, millennia ago. They will see us through today as they did before.

CHAPTER 1

The First Signposts

Who were the Celts?

In order to explore the practices of the druid shaman, we must first briefly clarify our definition of some familiar terms. The people from whom we get the term 'Celt', the *'Keltoi'* were first mentioned by the Greek historian Herodotus, as a group of people living in the region of the river Danube around 550BC. These people were distinctive in their incredible art, highly sophisticated culture, and material wealth. They were especially rich in gold. By this time it is believed that these people were a point of interchange with the Greeks, while also being part of a wider culture sharing common languages, customs and beliefs. These 'Celts' were an ethno-linguistic group of tribal Iron Age societies that spanned a large part of northern and western Europe as far as Britain and Ireland. They shared common values and traditions, with variations over time and from region to region. Contrary to popular belief, they were not a distinct genetic race, although some 'Celtic' customs and linguistic similarities survive today in most Celtic areas.

Britain, Cornwall, Wales, Scotland, the Isle of Man and Ireland are all considered to remain Celtic heartlands to this day, together with Brittany, and are often described with the term 'Insular Celts', as opposed to the 'Continental Celts'. These 'Insular Celts' diverged into the Gaelic Celts, of Ireland, Scotland and the Isle of Man, and the Brythonic Celts of Brittany, Cornwall and Wales. Scholars in the 19th and 20th centuries often argued that the Celts arrived in Britain via an invasion or succession of invasions around the 6th century BC from Continental Europe, but this has now been largely overturned due to a lack of archae-ological evidence, and the work of archaeologists such as Barry

Cunliffe.[2] The British Celts were for the most part probably the indigenous Britons, arriving in the early Bronze Age (2500BC) or even earlier, adopting and adapting Celtic culture due to their extensive relations and trading connections along the Atlantic seaboard and beyond.

These people are notoriously hard to pin down, although their cultural effects have been profound on later generations, creating a 'Celtic consciousness' and traditions that have spanned millennia, so that today much of Wales, Scotland and Ireland would still call themselves proudly 'Celtic' and often maintained practices which are distinctly Celtic in nature well into the modern era, such as those recorded by Alexander Carmichael in his *Carmina Gadelica* in the latter part of the 19th century.[3]

For the purposes of this book, the term Celtic is used in its widest and most common usage sense; primarily to refer to these British and Irish 'Celts' of the Iron Age as well as later Celts and Celtic practices spanning from them through Celtic Christianity to this day, with minor references to Iron Age Celtic Europe. This exploration of shamanic druidry, therefore, relates primarily to the traces of shamanic traditions as found in the British Isles and Ireland, translating their practice into forms applicable to today.

What is druidry? Who were and are the druids?

Druidry to some is a nature-based religion, to others it is a philosophy, a gentle way of life, focusing upon our relationship with nature. One thing that unites a lot of druids is a distrust of labels and categories; for some it is about researching, and reconstructing our Celtic past, for others it is about finding ways now, in the modern era, to reinvigorate our connection to the spirit in nature... and there are infinite variations. The druids of antiquity were Celtic priests, healers, seers and lore keepers, who worshipped the Celtic gods, and performed a wide variety of roles within the community. Today, not all druids worship gods of any kind, or do so outside of the Celtic tradition. However, a wide consensus would consider druidry today to find its roots, and certainly its spiritual aspirations, in the Celtic religious leaders of the Iron Age.

Most of what we know about the Celtic druids comes from Classical writers, although much can sensibly be gleaned from archaeological evidence as well. Caesar tells us that the home of the druid religion was in Britain[4] although traces of druidic practice are found across Celtic Europe, particularly in their sacred enclosures known as nemetons or groves. While some argue that druidry came to Britain via Europe, it is equally arguable that the spiritual beliefs of the indigenous tribes of Britain evolved and developed over time into the druidry of the Iron Age which expanded into the lands of the Continental Celts. Certainly great importance was placed upon the sacred spirit of the British landscape, which was honoured long before the arrival of Celtic culture.

The druids were divided into three groups, the *bards* of Wales and the *fili* of Ireland performing as oral historians and story-tellers of great magical significance, as well as the ovates, and the druid class themselves. Some of the greatest bardic works are attributed to the Welsh bard Taliesin, a deeply shamanic character, whose works reveal an ability to access the super-natural and knowledge of the spirit world. Both the bards and the Irish fili often appeared to perform tasks that were commonly held to be in the realm of the *ovates*, or soothsayers; uttering prophecy, giving advice or healings after going into trance states or forms of spiritual ecstasy, while the druid class themselves – who were judges, philosophers and astronomers, also appear to at times perform what may be understood today as shamanic practices... Their relationship with spirit, whether the gods, the ancestors or the spirits of the landscape, being central to their beliefs and activities, and the source of their knowledge and ability.

The word druid comes from the Indo-European root of the

word for oak, *'dru'* with that of the word for knowledge or wisdom *'wid'*, thus meaning *'those with the knowledge of the oak tree'*. It is also argued to come from *'deru-weid'* meaning someone with strong and steadfast wisdom and insight. It is possible that both these meanings are in fact closely entwined, having the steadfast strength of the oak, and the knowledge of 'seeing' or seership – a shamanic source of knowledge from spirit. The word survived into the Old Irish period giving us *druidecht* meaning 'magic' and in the Welsh as *dryw* meaning seer, which was a term used well into the 13th century.

What is a shaman?

A shaman is someone who reaches altered states of consciousness in order to encounter and interact with the spirit world. The term originates from the Tungusic and Samoyedic speaking peoples of North Asia, used to describe their magico-religious practitioners; but the term has spread today to describe those from cultures all around the world who act as intermediaries between the mortal world and the infinite, or the realm of spirit. Scholars now believe that most world religions have a basis in shamanic practice, going back as far as the Palaeolithic. Historian and philosopher Mircea Eliade called shamanism a *'technique of religious ecstasy'*; the shaman while encountering the world of spirit becomes a conduit for vast amounts of energy, direct from the Otherworld, or Source, to be used and applied in the mortal realm, for healing, guidance and to effect real change.

Shamanic practice

Central to shamanic practice is the interaction with spirits, both mortal and supernatural. Shamans believe we are all spirits made manifest in the mortal world, our wellbeing, health and wholeness stem from our connection with Source, and our own souls, just as a tree reaches upwards and outwards from the earth. When we are in a good state of wellness, we are continually renewed and strengthened by this connection. However, when this connection is weakened or partially disconnected (it can never be wholly severed) illness and imbalance result, our lives wander without a sense of purpose or fulfilment. Often in life someone will have a sense that something is 'missing' and this can be a sign that our connection to the deeper world of spirit via our own souls is not in a state of health. Often shamans talk of soul or power loss, which can result from all sorts of negative experiences. This has a profound effect on our lives and sense of self... we become disconnected and 'lost'; sometimes suffering illness or misfortune, or we find we feel we are lacking vitality, enthusiasm or inspiration. The shaman can restore this connection, returning lost soul parts, and vital power or life force. All illness and imbalance can be understood as stemming from the pre-manifest state of spirit, reaching manifestation in a person's body or general wellbeing, and the shaman may repair any damage by going direct to the source of the problem, with the resulting ripples in the manifest world returning health and wellbeing to the person in their everyday life.

Yet shamanic work goes far beyond this, as someone who is primarily in service with spirit, shamanic work also entails caring for nature and all beings, our environment and community, as well as the pursuit of health, wholeness and spiritual evolution within ourselves. This is not separate from shamanic healing, but in fact all part of the same tasks and activities. By interacting with the spirit world and aligning and reconnecting oneself with the whole of creation, we naturally heal and effect healing in others, as well as grow and develop along our own soul's journey. The end result of this is enlightenment, expressed in the Celtic tradition as the attainment of bardic inspiration, revealed as the 'radiant brow' of shaman poets such as Taliesin and the expansive knowledge of all things he shares with key characters of Celtic myth, such as *Finn Mac Cumhaill* and *Tuan Mac Cairill*. Prioritising care for all beings, especially nature, is also key to most druidic practice today.

Celtic shamans

The term 'Celtic shaman' is a modern one, utilising the modern understanding of both 'Celtic' and 'shaman' and thus viewing the practices of the Iron Age druids and earlier, through a 21st century lens. However, while it is impossible to ever know the Iron Age druids and their beliefs and practices from their point of view, we can draw sensible and logical conclusions extrapolating from what we do know, even if we are aware they may have used different names and terms of reference for their activities. If we turn ourselves away from historical reconstruction and archaeology for a moment, and also consider that our relationship with the unseen and the world of spirit is just as much our birthright as theirs, then we may also access the spirits of our lands, the gods, and the Otherworld, and using their examples, experience it through our own senses, through our own eyes. The old roads may be less trodden today, but they still remain, for those prepared to follow the trail once again.

A guide on the path...Taliesin

Taliesin, meaning 'radiant brow', was perhaps the greatest shaman poet of Britain. *Taliesin Pen Beirdd* is a historical character, living in Wales in the 6th century, composing many songs and poems which survive in various forms to this day. Many were rediscovered in the 18th century and translated from Welsh into English with varying forms of success. However, the title 'radiant brow' was for a time often misunderstood, and it is now a common belief that while some poems are the work of the 6th century poet, others are part of an oral history recorded at that time, but originating centuries earlier, referring to beliefs and practices of a far older date. 'Radiant brow' is thus a description or title, rather than a personal name.

The figure of Taliesin has a mythical beginning, recorded in the 16th century manuscript *Hanes Taliesin* as the boy Gwion Bach, who was set to serve the Lady/Goddess Ceridwen by attending to her Cauldron of Inspiration, which was brewing a magical potion to give her son, Morfran, knowledge and wisdom beyond all men. Yet three drops of the brew spilled out and burnt Gwion, who sucked at his fingers, and received the potion's magic instead. (This is also a key feature in the tale of Finn and the salmon of knowledge.) He is then pursued by the terrible and fearsome Goddess, both Gwion and Ceridwen undergoing numerous shape-changes, until he becomes a grain of wheat, and she a hen who eats him. Ceridwen is then pregnant with the boy Gwion, and when she gives birth to him, this being Gwion's second birth, she is so struck by his beauty that she cannot bear to hurt him, but places him inside a leather bag upon the sea. Gwion is finally found, by the Lord Elffin on the shore of the river Conwy, while he is fishing for salmon (a symbol of wisdom). Thus Gwion is reborn a third time when he is brought forth from the bag, Elffin naming him Taliesin upon seeing his great radiance. Able to utter prophecy, and recite poetry with magical effect from birth, Taliesin is one of many 'wondrous children' in Celtic myth, marking them out as beings of both the mortal realm and the Otherworld.

Here we see Taliesin is three times born, as a mortal, then from the womb of the Goddess, before a final birth out into the world where he serves as chief poet and magical ally (shaman) to Elffin, and later at King Arthur's court. This is a shamanic initiation seen through the eyes of myth, with its shape-changing, animal embodiments, and divine interactions before being cast upon the great ocean of spirit, to come into relationship with the whole of creation itself. This is every shaman's task and objective.

CHAPTER 2

Preparing for Voyage

Within the crane skin bag – a druid's shamanic tools

The crane skin bag is a perennial motif in several Celtic myths. Originally it was made from the magical skin of the Goddess Aoife, who spent many years as a crane – a bird able to travel between the worlds. When she died, her husband, the sea God Mannanan, made the special bag in order to store the great treasures of the land, known as the hallows, within it. This can be understood as symbolising the great powers of the land, and the tools of the soul, as residing within the womb of the Goddess, Lady Sovereignty herself, who goes under many names.

The crane skin bag was then passed to the hero Cumhail, and then to his son, the shaman hero Fionn mac Cumhail, who held these talismans of the earth's power in protection and guardianship of the land and its sacred soul, after tasting the 'salmon of knowledge' which gave him almost super human powers. Later traditions used the motif of the crane skin bag, as a pouch or container in which to store magical tools, herbs and other items of spiritual or magical significance.

This is still a term used by druids today, and it is possible to buy or make your own 'crane skin' bag, of cloth or leather, in which to store things which you use in your practice – stones, feathers, herbs, as well as other druidic or shamanic tools. We will now look over some 'shamanic' tools which may help you in your practice. While none of them are necessary, they are nonetheless very helpful in assisting your gentle change of consciousness, and should not be immediately overlooked.

A druid shaman doesn't need a lot of equipment. There is a temptation to go out and buy lovely tools, indeed there are some beautiful drums, rattles and other tools on the market these days, but it should be said that these objects, over time, become just as much your allies and power sources as your spirit guides and guardians. For this reason it is always best to make your own tools if you can, or at least customise, decorate, bless and consecrate them yourself. The aim is to build a relationship with the spirit of your tools, and to empower and energise them through respect and good use. This is much easier done when you have put your own energy into its construction or birth.

The shaman's drum

A drum is an excellent and really versatile shamanic tool. It can be used to help you and others reach into meditative or trance states for journeying, and the skill of drumming a regular rhythm for a length of time teaches presence, intent and the kind of relaxed focus that is central to shamanic work of all kinds. Drumming can be used in ceremony, as an energy raiser, as a voice of spirit, as an invoker and as a gift to the spirits. It can be used in healing, to shake and raise the vibration of a person or area, to clear and energise, dislodging stuck or negative energy. It can create atmospheres and assist in directing will and intention, by beating fast or slow, it can motivate a climb to the upperworld, or echo a flock of birds taking flight, it can slow and relax, and become the heartbeat of the earth.

The drum is the shaman's friend, almost more than any other. They come in so many shapes and sizes; the traditional Irish bodhran is great for Celtic shamanic use, but you needn't feel that an Irish drum is compulsory. Take your time, and find a design that works well for you, that feels right, that excites your enthusiasm.

Rattles

Rattles are another excellent shamanic tool. Like the drum, the rattle can be used to alter consciousness, build energy, evoke, banish negative energy, and for healing, but its energy is quite different, faster and lighter, its effects are often subtler. Rattles are particularly useful when working with nature spirits, wind and rain. Gourds make excellent natural rattles, and ones filled with seeds are very good for blessing new growth, or encouraging the patter of rain upon dry ground. Antlers, sticks and bones are also useful percussive tools, and can be very powerful, often drawing upon the spirit of the material used to construct them.

Flutes and whistles

Some shamans like to work with flutes, whistles or other wind instruments, and these are especially useful for working with air spirits, although nature spirits of all kinds are attracted by them. How they are worked with varies from instrument to instrument and person to person. Entering into a sacred, meditative state of mind, and playing it, is the best way to discover its spirit and uses, being open to its voice and the inspiration of spirit.

Shawls, veils and eye masks

Having some sort of blanket, hood, cloth or eye mask to cover the head when journeying is very useful, to cut out light and distractions. Having something to lie on can also be useful; traditionally a bull's hide was used specifically for this in a darkened hut. Celtic shamans do not always lie down when working, and highland seers recorded in folklore journeyed while sitting with their eyes open – a skill that comes with practice, and is far more effective than lying down, where we may drift to sleep, or lose our focus as we get too relaxed. However, we know that druids did lie down in specially made structures in order to receive vision and, these days, lying down is the most common technique. So, if you feel you need to, try to find a blanket or shawl that you can use specifically for your shamanic work, alone or in addition to something to cover your head and eyes. This will also be your ally and working friend, building power with use.

The silver branch

The silver branch is something which features in several Irish myths, and is traditionally used to invoke and gain access to the Otherworld. Today many Celtic shamans work with the silver branch, but it is not something to make as a beginner, and certainly not something to buy. It is rather for use when a good level of experience has been achieved. As a powerful symbol as well as magical tool, it will work best when the spirits feel you have a certain deeper level of contact, and have shown them enough respect not to rush the process.

The shaman's shield

Shamans sometimes like to work with shields, which they can use to decorate their space, and invoke the spirits of their allies, via the spirits' physical representations upon the shield itself. Animal allies are often painted upon shields for this purpose, and can be used for protection. They can also be carried in spirit while journeying, again used for protection and empowerment. Alder shields were used by Celtic warriors, the red of the cut wood providing magical power, and showing the tree had sacrificed itself in the place of the warrior thus insuring their protection. Rowan also has highly protective magical qualities, and both are very suitable together with hazel and willow, which may be easier to use. Shamans' shields needn't be made of solid wood, and can be a wooden frame made of a thin alder, rowan, hazel or willow branch, covered with cloth or paper. This can then be decorated with things that represent the shamans' allies, whether that is a painted picture, symbols, feathers or shells tied on with ribbon. Allow the shield's construction to be a creative, spirit-inspired project, that reflects your particular nature and way of working, as well as your allies and guardians.

Blessing and befriending your tools

When you have made or bought your drum, rattle, flute, shawl, shield, or other tool, create a simple ceremony to befriend it and bless it. Make time and space to play it or be with it for an hour. Notice all its small details. If it is a musical instrument, get to know all the different tones it can make, and for drums decide whether you want to use a beater or your hand, or both depending on the occasion. Speak to it as an ally and friend, and welcome it to your home. Pass it through some incense or sprinkle lightly with some spring water, and ask that the spirit of your tool be cleansed and blessed by all good spirits, or your chosen gods. Burning dried mugwort or vervain are very good incenses for the Celtic shaman's use.

In time, you will notice that your way of working with your tool evolves. Occasionally with your musical tools you will notice a change in their voice as they work with you. Always do your best to heed the voice of your instrument, however subtle the changes, and it will be a great ally.

Power and the soul – the 'fire in the head'

One of the central aspects of the shaman's work is the wellbeing of the soul. This core, energised eternal aspect of our selves, that goes beyond our personality and everyday activities and awareness, can be understood as our divine spark, our infinite self, that by its very nature is constantly in connection to Source. This is the animating force within our physical bodies. It is the soul which continues before and after death, and travels the roads of spirit when a shaman journeys to the Otherworld. The ability to see and communicate with spirits, often called 'seership' in the Celtic tradition, may also be understood as soul-sight; seeing not only the physical appearance, but the soul or spirit within.

The soul functions as our main connection to Source, and vivifies and empowers us and our path through life. In some ways, it is Source made manifest, exploring and unfolding via creation, as the Self or individual. When a person is in a good relationship with their own soul, their lives reflect this inner wellbeing, and the path they take in life will in some measure follow the path that their soul and inner knowing desires for them. In general terms, physical and emotional health, and a well-rounded productive life follows as a result. Connection to soul results in wholeness and balance. However, there are many obstacles along this path in the mortal realm, and today's modern world allows little space for listening and following our inner promptings, and fostering a relationship with our soul. There have always been challenges to this in one form or another, resulting in conditions commonly understood in shamanic terms as soul or power loss.

By retrieving, reclaiming or realigning to our soul and source of power, we can return to wholeness and health in all the spheres of our life; mental, emotional, physical and practical. Yet this has the potential to go beyond a basic level of wellbeing, into a state of full connection and empowerment – an alignment with the divine and a state of enlightenment. This connection and reconnection to our power can be understood as the 'radiant brow' of Taliesin, and what W.B. Yeats refers to in his poem *The Song of Wandering Aengus:*

I went out into the hazel wood
Because a fire was in my head...

This 'fire' inspires Aengus to go fishing for trout, another way of referring to the mythical beast, the Salmon of Knowledge, a source of this wholeness and soul connection, an embodiment of the source of bardic or shamanic wisdom. When he returns home, the trout transforms into a beautiful maiden, who runs out through the door, leading Aengus to endlessly travel *'through hollow lands and hilly lands'* in search of her. This can be seen as the shaman's journey, questing through the realms of spirit in search of the soul.

This fire or radiance in the head or brow, is a sign that the spirit body or soul is fully empowered and full of life force, drawn from Source. A similar concept can be seen in Kundalini yoga, where the life force, or Kundalini, is drawn in to the body with the aim of it rising up through the various energy systems, until it rises through the crown at the top of the head. Kundalini means 'coiled' and is considered to be like a coiled serpent, residing in the lower spine. To the Celts, the serpent held similar significance, representing the earthy physical energy of life force, but also fertility, wisdom and immortality, health and healing. A horned serpent was a common symbol of divine authority – that is, the 'serpent' within was significantly raised within the body through the energy systems known in the Celtic tradition as 'the three cauldrons', (from the medieval Irish poem The Cauldron of Poesy) and thus enlightenment was attained, resulting in the 'radiant brow'.

Raising energy and power – the tree posture

This posture is a key exercise for use with the other exercises mentioned in this book, and is used to raise energy within the body, for use in journeying and other shamanic practices. It utilises earth and sky/heaven as well as the worlds of above and below as vehicles for connection to Source, and will fill up your energy field with power for you to use. There are many variations on this basic principle, and repeated use is good for general wellbeing and connection to our divine selves, keeping us as aligned as possible with our souls. It will also assist us in building our 'psychic muscles' increasing our abilities with steady practise. Its basis is the horned figure in the Gunderstrup Cauldron, commonly understood to be the god Cernunnos, or a figure with a horned headdress, perhaps invoking and embodying him; the antlers illustrating his raised life force and enlightened shamanic state of consciousness. It echoes another important and powerful symbol in the Celtic tradition, the tree; connected to the earth below, with arms raised into the heavens, like branches, yet still and poised, in a state of energised and healthy tension between the upper and underworld. It is therefore fully activated, conscious and present in physical manifest reality as a result.

Exercise 1: The tree posture

Sit with crossed legs, as comfortably as possible. If you are unable to hold this position for long, hold it as long as you can without injury, allowing a certain amount of tension in your position to help hold the energy in your body and energy field.

Take three deep breaths then, sitting with your back straight, visualise yourself growing a tail, or tap root, down from the base of your spine, into the earth. Visualise this root or tail growing deeper and deeper towards the heart of the earth. See the deep fiery heart of the earth beneath you like a great star, an embodiment of Source, supplying endless energy and connection. Now with every out-breath see your root or tail growing deeper, and with every in-breath, visualise yourself drawing up energy from the earth, like warm golden and green light. Slowly it rises up your body into your legs and lower back, up your hips and waist, and up your spine. This is the trunk of your tree. As the energy rises further, slowly raise your upper arms, and then your lower arms, with your elbows at right angles, until your upper arms are level with your shoulders, at your sides, opening your chest area. As the energy rises further into your upper chest, shoulders and throat, raise your lower arms so your hands are at the same level as your head. These are your branches. Continue to raise the energy with every in-breath, until you visualise it swirling around your brow and the crown of your head. Keep your hands at head height as long as is comfortable to hold the energy in your head and to stop it from rising further up into the heavens.

Now gently turn your attention to above you, and visualise white starry light from the heavens descending towards you, naturally attracted to the earth energy you have raised, just as the Gods of the sky are drawn to the Goddesses of the earth. This energy descends into your brow, merging and swirling with the energy from below, and descending further until it merges and settles within the centre of your chest.

Hold this state of raised energy, balanced between earth and sky, with your back straight, the trunk of your tree strong, rooted to earth, but also connected to the stars, via your braches and twigs, right to the tips of your fingers. Breathe deep and slow, taking your time, for as long as you can without any physical

injury, before thanking the heavens, and visualising the star energy retreat, and gently lowering your arms. Gently turn your attention to your root or tail. Thank the earth, and gently retract your energy from the earth, until you are returned fully into your body.

This exercise can be performed alone or as precursor to journeying or other shamanic work.

CHAPTER 3

Circle Time

The Celtic wheel of the year

Now that we have explored tools and druidic shamanic techniques of power raising, we must turn our attention to positioning our practice within space and time. We do this through the medium of the circle, which functions not only as a delineation for sacred space, but also as vehicle for travelling within time via the wheel of the seasons. By aligning ourselves with the motif and energy of the turning sun, and the spinning earth, we position our work in relation to these cycles of cosmological health and balance.

The Celts divided the year into two halves, the warm and the cold, subdivided into roughly four parts, corresponding with the four seasons each marked by special festivals. They can, if we wish, then be divided further by the solstices and equinoxes, providing us with a calendar of eight festivals, now commonly known as the wheel of the year. Some festivals had particular prominence in certain communities across the Celtic lands, and it seems very few if any celebrated all eight. However, these eight dates have significance predating the Celts and go back into the Neolithic – many monuments dating from then are aligned to various festivals on the wheel. At least one stone circle, Castlerigg, has stones marking the positions of all eight, suggesting that the tradition of the wheel goes back very far indeed.

The eight festivals of the wheel of the year are as follows:

Imbolc 'ewe's milk'– February 2nd

Literally meaning 'ewe's milk', Imbolc celebrates the birth of the lambs, and the first signs of spring, however scarce. The gift of ewe's milk was essential to get the very young old or sickly through the last weeks of winter, and was a sign of the Mother Goddess's beneficence. The festival is sacred to the fire Goddess Brighid, who oversees childbirth and is Goddess of hearth and home, as well as smith craft, healing and poetry. Brighid was said to overturn winter by defeating or transforming from the Cailleach, or old woman of winter.

Spring Equinox – approx March 21st

A time of equal day and night, and the first real days of spring, the Spring Equinox marks the point where the days are getting markedly longer and warmer. Although there may have once been a Celtic Goddess of the spring, now forgotten, today it is commonly a time to honour the Germanic and Saxon lunar Goddess Eostre or Ostara, whose sacred symbols of the hare and the egg were adapted into the imagery of the Christian Easter.

Beltane 'the good fire' – May 1st

This major fire festival is the counterpoint to Samhain. It is a time of burgeoning life and fertility, celebrating the sacred sexual union of the Goddess and God. The Sun God Bel presides over this festival, and has been considered as part of a divine couple with the Goddess Danu, although different areas of the Celtic world may have favoured other gods and goddesses at this time.

Summer Solstice – approx June 21st

The longest day, celebrated in cultures all over the world, where the fertility of the earth and the power of the sun is at its height. It is the natural counterpoint to the Winter Solstice, whose importance is marked in so many Neolithic monuments._

Lughnasadh 'the feast of Lugh' or 'the commemoration of Lugh'– August 1st

'The commemoration of Lugh' was a time of massive gatherings, feasts, competitions, markets and legal proceedings, where the whole tribe got together to attend to the business of trading and resolving disputes. The festival is sacred to the Solar God Lugh, who oversees both legal matters and the attainment of skill and prowess, and his foster mother the Earth Goddess Tailtiu, whom Lugh commemorated at this time for her sacrifice in clearing the plains of Ireland for agriculture.

Autumn Equinox – approx September 21st

Day and night are equal once more, but the nights are drawing in and winter approaches. This is a time of harvest and seed gathering and sowing. The Sun God is descending into the underworld, to return reborn at the Winter Solstice.

Samhain 'summer's end' – October 31st

'Summer's end', or Samhain, is a feast of the dead. The Sun God has retreated entirely into the underworld, and with him the souls of the dead. It is a time to honour the ancestors, and all that has passed and, in the depths of the night, to await the new life that is to come. This is the time to explore the underworld Annwn.

Winter Solstice – approx December 21st

The longest night and the shortest day, honoured in Britain particularly in the Neolithic era, when many barrow mounds were aligned to the first rays of the Winter Solstice sun. The sun has completed its descent and is once again on the rise from this point.

Seasonal patterns

These eight festivals form a never-ending circular pattern of increase and decline, life and death, that mirror not only the seasons, but the spiritual and mortal life. They also reflect the turning of the sun, and the waxing and waning of the moon, and can be understood as turning in a circular clockwise pattern around the four directions of north, east, south and west, just as the stars do around the pole.

Thus we have Imbolc in the north-east, representing the very first stirring of life and the spring, hidden but emerging into the world. Then we have Spring Equinox in the east, the dawn of the year, where new life bursts forth, leading on to Beltane in the south-east, as the days grow warmer and the earth becomes fertile. In the south we find the Summer Solstice, the fertility of the land and of our lives grown to maturity. This leads on to the south-west and Lughnasadh, where we reach perhaps the height of skill and ability, and the earth is birthing a great harvest of abundance for us to enjoy. This harvest continues into the Autumn Equinox in the west, where we discover that we always reap what we sow, and feel the first hints of age and winter to come. At Samhain, positioned in the north-west, old age and death arrive as the world turns to the coming winter, and the veil thins, revealing the spirit world that lies beyond. In the north, at the Winter Solstice, the world turns to ice, to silence and stillness, and the mortal discovers that life comes out of death, lying in the tomb and womb of the Earth Goddess. This is the pivotal point, where the possibilities and potential of new life transform from the old and the dead, and await the new life to come as Imbolc approaches once again...

The Celts had a highly complex calendar, which is in fact so amazingly accurate that it takes 19 years to go full circle. Its knowledge was lost for millennia until the discovery of the Coligny Calendar, which was found in Coligny, near Lyons, in France, in 1897. Engraved on a bronze tablet dating from the end of the second century AD, sigils marked the festivals of Beltane and Lughnasadh, and each year began at Samhain.

The Coligny Calendar overlays our modern Roman Calendar into the following months:

Samonios: 'Seed fall' or *month of assembly* – Oct/Nov

Dumannios: 'Darkest depths' or *month of sacred smoke* – Nov/Dec

Riuros: 'Cold-time' or *fatten up month* – Dec/Jan

Anagantios: 'Stay at home time', or *month where no one travels* – Jan/Feb

Ogronios: 'Time of ice' or *freezing month* – Feb/Mar

Cutios: 'Time of winds' – Mar/Apr

Giamonios: 'Shoots show' or *month of the yearling calves* – Apr/May

Samivisionos: 'Time of brightness' or *month of sun* – May/June

Equos: 'Horse time' – June/July

Elembiuos: 'Claim time' or *month of the deer* – July/Aug

Edrinios: 'Arbitration time' or *month of heat* – Aug/Sept

Cantlos: 'Song time' – Sept/Oct[5]

As you can see, the names of these months are based on agricultural and cultural events – over all, our understanding of the Celtic year should be primarily practical and experiential. Based on an innate connection with the world around us, living with similar values, reverence for knowledge and tradition, but also embracing adaptation and innovation just as they would, we can make it relevant for us today.

The four directions

The never-ending spiral around the year and the seasons is mirrored by and due to the planets' never-ending spin around the sun, and the wheeling stars. A druid shaman navigates and orientates him/herself through this world, and the Otherworld of spirit, by developing a deep sense of centredness and presence throughout this eternal spiral, by becoming, in a sense, the axis mundi, the central pole around which the wheel spins. Movement and other engagement with the spirit world is thus based on positioning oneself within the four directions of north, east, south and west, or ahead, behind, to the right and left. In addition there is also, of course, above, below and within.

Each of these four directions is in turn traditionally related to each of the four major elements, earth, air, wind and fire, and a final fifth – spirit, which in turn vivifies all the other four. Thus the north is related to the element of earth; the east, air; the south, fire; and the west, water. These are drawn from the four magical cities of the Irish gods the Tuatha de Danann; Gorias, Finnias, Murias and Falias respectively.

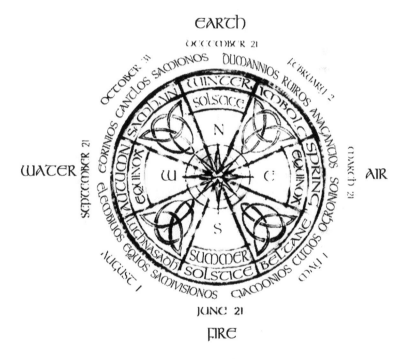

Directional and elemental spirits and faeries

The four directions, with their associated festivals, seasons and elements also give rise to further correspondences. In addition, their accompanying spirit beings, sometimes known as elementals, have their own qualities and traditional names from Classical tradition. There are also numerous spirits named and remembered in Celtic folkloric knowledge and mythology, some of which are known as faeries, or the Sidhe, who also have elemental associations. Many of these are suitable allies for the druid shaman and may be called upon for assistance. There are also animals related to the directions which can be called upon.

Here is a selection of these correspondences and some of their accompanying spirits:

North: Earth, winter, tomb/womb, wisdom, practicality, materialism, manifestation, stillness. Elementals: Classical tradition – Gnomes. Celtic – Brownies, knockers. Animal – Bear.

East: Air, spring, birth, youth, ideas, inspiration, communication, intellect, movement. Elementals: Classical tradition – Sylphs. Celtic – Spriggans, Animal – Hawk.

South: Fire, summer, maturity, sexuality, energy, skill, accomplishment, leadership, expansion. Elementals: Classical tradition – Salamanders. Celtic – Ellylldan, hearth spirits. Animal – Stag.

West: Water, autumn, age, emotions, dreams, vision, psychic abilities, imagination, simplification. Elementals: Classical tradition – Nymphs. Celtic – kelpies, selkies. Animal – Salmon.

Creating Sacred Space

For almost all druidic or shamanic practice, it is essential to create sacred space. This can be as simple as having a clear, calm area in which to work that is conducive to a meditative state, or it can be a complicated magical circle in which negative spirits or energies are 'banished' and positive or helpful spirits are 'invoked'. However, not all magical circles need to be complicated to create, and it is possible to make a sacred space within a circle quite easily.

The circle is the perfect space for spiritual and magical work, as it has two main functions inherent in its shape and design.

Firstly, it creates a boundary, a clearly delineated and protected line between what goes on inside the circle, and what remains outside. The other is key to how it works... as a circle it mirrors the energetic pattern created by all of creation, that of the spinning circle or spiral. In one sense this creates a sacred space via echoing in microcosm this larger, in fact universal, pattern. Yet it also creates an energetic pattern in itself that is so compatible with this natural flow as to build its power and energy from the natural forces that surround it, converting it to our use.

Exercise 2: Circle casting

This simple exercise is a good way to create a sacred circle space, and orient yourself within the four directions, and the four elements. It is a good place to start if you are new to this practice, and can have other things added to it as you progress. It is also perfect for use when shamanic journeying, without being unduly ceremonial.

You will need one candle.

First prepare your space. This may be as simple as having a bit of a tidy, so you are not distracted, and creating a pleasant atmosphere.

Place your candle somewhere central in your space, together with matches or a lighter. You may like to place objects relating to the four elements in their relevant quarter, or an altar, but this isn't essential.

Next prepare yourself. Take three deep breaths and calm and centre yourself. Stand in the middle of your sacred space, and then turn your attention to drawing in energy from deep within the earth. (See Exercise 1: The tree posture.) With each breath, visualise the energy rising up your body, filling you with light. Slowly raise your arms as the energy rises, so that it flows to just above your head. You may then choose to visualise light descending to you from above, settling in your chest area. When you are ready gently lower your arms, so as to be comfortable.

Turn to the east. This is the direction of the air, the spring, the dawn, the time of youth and inspiration. The animal related to this direction in the Celtic tradition is the hawk. Focus on these aspects… do you feel more drawn to the east as a direction, or its element, air, or its qualities, spirits, or its animal? Or all of these? Visualise a simple doorway in front of you, and beyond, the energies of the east, and all its associations. Open your arms wide in invocation, see the door open, and call out to the east to join you and to assist you with your work or meditation. Try these or your own words: *'Spirits of the east, and the air, hawk of the dawn, I call to you, join me in this sacred place, in kinship and blessing.'*

Then using one arm, point your index finger towards the east and, feeling the energy still rising up from the earth (down from the sky too if you like), 'draw' the line of the circle from the east to the south. Visualise the energy rising up and along your arm, drawing the line in golden light. You may have to take a few steps depending on the size of your space, so the central candle remains roughly in the middle of your circle.

Turn to the south. This is the direction of the fire, of summer, adulthood, and power. The animal related to this direction is the stag. Focus on these aspects… do you feel more drawn to the south as a direction, or its element, fire, or its qualities, spirits, or its animal? Or all of these? Again visualise a simple doorway in front of you, and beyond, the energies of the south and all its associations. Open both your arms wide in invocation, see the door open, and call out to the south to join you and to assist you with your work or meditation. Try these or your own words: *'Spirits of the south, and the fire, stag of the noon day sun, I call to you, join me in this sacred place, in kinship and blessing.'*

Now lower your other arm again and, visualising the flow of energy, continue to draw the circle along to the west.

The west is the direction of water, autumn, evening, the time of dreaming and vision. The animal related to the west is the salmon of wisdom, who as an animal related to water, is also connected to the emotions, and the heart. Again, focus on these qualities… what about them attracts you the most? Visualise the door of the west ahead of you, opening, and beyond all the energies of the west, and ask them to join you. Again, try these or your own words: *'Spirits of the west, and the waters, salmon of wisdom, of the gloaming, I call to you, join me in this sacred place, in kinship and blessing.'*

Lower your other arm again and, visualising the flow of energy, this time continue to draw the circle along to the north.

The north is the place of earth, winter, death and rebirth. The animal related to the north is the bear, who hibernates in the winter, thus living between the worlds, and whose star brother, the great bear constellation, dwells in the northern sky. Focus on these things, and finally, visualise the door of the north before you, opening as you invoke the energies of the north. Say: *'Spirits of the north, and the deep earth, great bear of the night, I call to you, join me in this sacred place, in kinship and blessing.'*

Continue to draw your circle, round one final quarter from the north to the east. Pause a moment, and see the circle as complete, whole, and powerful. Does the circle stay static? Or does it spin gently? How does it feel?

You have now invoked the four quarters, and your circle is guarded and blessed by the elemental powers themselves.

With practise you can perfect your own way of casting a circle. Sometimes you may choose full invocations of the four directions, and at others you may simply choose to 'draw' your circle with energy. Alternatively you may prefer to invoke the quarters without drawing a circle at all. Learn to feel the energy of both the space and the quarters, so that you can use these techniques and relate to these things in a way that is relevant to you personally.

Lighting the candle

When you are ready, you may choose to light a candle in the centre of your circle. This functions as your axis mundi, the central hub of your wheel, which transcends the horizontal axis of your circle, ascending and descending into the other worlds, above and below. It represents the world tree, the crossroads, the faery well, and your access to 'Source'.

You have now created a sacred space in which to perform ceremony, or druid shamanic journeying. Within this space, you may choose to raise further energy through drumming, rattling or chanting.

When you are ready, close down you sacred space by thanking all the beings you have called to you, in reverse order, and returning the energy to earth and sky.

CHAPTER 4

Setting Out

The first journeys or voyages of a druid shaman are to gain primary allies which will give support and tuition along the path. The forms these allies take are varied, but for the purposes of this book we shall first seek a druid shaman ally, to function as guide, protector and teacher, and an ancestral ally, one who is associated specifically with your ancestral bloodline, who knows you and your path in intimate detail, and can be beneficial for personal healing.

The grove – finding a druid shaman ally

A druid shaman ally can function as many things, a guide and a protector, as well as a teacher. They are your primary contact point in the spirit world, who can see things from your point of view. Most other types of ally are helpful because of their difference to the shaman. They offer a different perspective and skill set, but your druid shaman ally will be a spirit who has walked this path before you, and understands the terrain upon which you wander from a mortal human perspective. They can give insights into your daily practice, assisting you in your work like any other ally, but also give you a link in the spirit world to others who have worked in this way before you. They differ from an ancestral ally, as they are not necessarily of your bloodline, or concerned with your family patterns. Instead they are guardians of tradition and skill, holding the knowledge and frequency of druidry and druidic shamanism, to pass on via shamanic communion and interchange.

For this reason the druid shaman ally is usually human in form, although their advanced stage of development may have altered various features depending on their own callings and inclinations. These will most likely be compatible with the fine subtleties of your own interests and eventual way of working. Thus they may have many supernatural seeming attributes, in addition to their general spirit form. They may have flaming eyes; appear to be part tree or animal, or even have stellar or off-world qualities impossible to describe. However, their most abiding quality will be a distinct human or humanoid 'feeling' about them. Once they were human just like you. The same will go for the time in which they lived and worked. Some will be drawing upon experiences in our far Mesolithic past, or even earlier, with very wild, ritualistic shamanic ways, while some, who lived in Bronze Age or Iron Age times, may have a more ceremonial druidic way of working, or a blend of the two. Some guides may even appear to be of more recent times.

The guide that comes to you will be the right one for you at this time. There is no right or wrong in this, no one guide is better than another. The two of you will form a unique combination capable of creating exactly the right circumstances, events and spirit contacts that are appropriate for you personally. You will learn the skills you need and have access to the right spirit connections as a result. We always start where we are, and the guides and allies that come to us are always perfect for our unique position in the web.

Exercise 3: Finding your druid shaman ally

First create your sacred space then, sitting comfortably, calm and centre yourself with three deep breaths. Raise your energy from the earth until your body is filled with light, slowly raising your arms before visualising light descending from above, and finally lowering your arms again. (See Exercise 1: The tree posture.)

When you are ready, visualise an oak door ahead of you, and lower your arms so as to be comfortable. Remember to keep your back straight, and your breathing steady, deep and even. Focus on the door, and affirm to yourself your intention to seek your druid shaman ally.

Go up to the door, feel its smooth close oak grain beneath your fingers. This is a manifestation of the great oak, lord of the strong door. Know that you travel under the oak's protection and guidance. Take note of any details on the door. Are there any markings? Runes? Ogham? Other symbols? If there are, focus on them, so you can hold them in your memory for when you have returned. Do you know their meaning? Contemplate them a moment before crossing over.

As you step through you see you are in a vast forest. There are two huge oak trees on either side of you, marking the beginning of a path through the trees. These are guardians of your way. On this occasion you must stick to the path, and they will ensure your success. You walk on through the trees.

Eventually you come to a clearing, circled by tall trees, and carpeted with soft green grass and fallen leaves. Gentle sunlight streams through the canopy above you, and the wind stirs, creating a gentle rattle of wooden chimes in the branches hidden a little further off. This is a sacred grove, a nemeton, functioning as a safe Otherworldly destination for you to work in from this point onwards. As you step into the clearing you feel a distinct change of atmosphere, as if the air itself tingles or is mildly electrical. It is not unpleasant and as you step forward the feeling settles and calms within you. In the centre of the clearing there is a fire, its flames spitting and hissing and crackling in the sunlight. Next to the fire is a person, sitting calmly.

You now approach the fire, and the sitting figure. As you get nearer you notice all sorts of things seem to hang in the branches of the trees around you; bones, feathers, red ribbons, small wicker structures, but other than the fire, there is nothing but the person in the clearing itself. Take a moment to notice their features, and greet them politely. You may feel certain that this is your guide, but you can ask them to confirm this if you wish. Take a few minutes to get acquainted as you would with any stranger. Be bold, and walk around them, seeing them from all angles. Allow yourself to be curious, and allow them to be curious about you in return. Take time to look each other in the eye especially. Be confident in yourself and your instincts. How do they seem to you? Do you trust them?

This is the first stage in a long and productive friendship. Stay by the fire with your guide for as long as you are able, just getting to know them. Your instruction with them will probably begin quite quickly, and it's OK to ask questions. However, the most important details are to make a good clear contact, so that you can find them again. They may have a name they wish to share, though don't push them on this, or they may have a symbol or object you can use to call them and connect with them in future.

When you are ready, thank them, and return along the path back to the two oak trees and the oak door. They may return to the door with you or say goodbye at the clearing. Either way, at this stage, do not cross the doorway with them, but part in the Otherworld.

When you are ready, cross back through the door. Take your time before opening your eyes, and gently return to everyday consciousness. Begin by clenching and unclenching your hands, and wiggling your toes, before moving your body. Close down your sacred space when you are ready. Remember to ground yourself well afterwards, with eating and drinking. Record your experiences in a journal if you wish.

You will find it productive to regularly repeat this exercise and meditate within your grove, or simply 'be' and commune with your guide there. This is your personal space within the Otherworld, which you can return to, in order to refresh and renew yourself and draw in energy or insight, or contact your druid shaman ally for further guidance.

The ancestral council fire

Ancestral allies, although often overlooked, are probably the most useful for our own personal journeys through life. So much that we do and experience in life is down to our original circumstances, where we were born, and to whom. These form a long chain of often very similar life stories, reflecting and responding to one another in an endless dance of cause and effect. So many things are carried along to us through this dance; patterns of behaviour, conscious and unconscious as well as cultural and emotional, are passed along together with our DNA and the family photos. They are part of a legacy that we both inherit and embody for good or ill.

An ancestral ally is usually someone who lived much further down the line, who has chosen to help those of the same blood. Remember on one level our family ancestors and bloodlines go back millennia, to before we were humans even, and ultimately right back to the beginning of the universe. Thus an ancestral ally may have any of a hundred forms, or more. However, the spiritual impulse in them has led them to choose to befriend and support family members with whom they have a sense of resonance. They will have faced many of the same challenges that feature in your personal story, and overcome them. As a result they are excellent for help with healing and empowerment, as well as overturning old or outworn ways of being.

Exercise 4: Finding your ancestral ally

First create your sacred space, and sitting comfortably, calm and centre yourself with three deep breaths. Then raise your energy from the earth until your body is filled with light, slowly raising your arms into the tree posture (see exercise 1: the tree posture). When you are ready, visualise an oak door ahead of you, and lower your arms so as to be comfortable. Remember to keep your back straight, and your breathing steady deep and even. Focus on the door, and affirm to yourself your intention to seek your ancestral ally.

When you are ready, step through the doorway. On the other

side you find you are standing on the path through the dense forest. There are two oak trees on either side of you; these are your guardians on this journey. Follow the path through the trees. You may pass your sacred grove, but carry on, and gradually the landscape rises, and you see the path is leading you clockwise around a steep craggy hill.

Suddenly you see before you a low cave entrance has opened up into the hillside. On your left, below you, is a gentle stream which has carved its way through the rocks, its source being deep in the hill before you. You approach the cave's entrance, and see the flickering light and shadow of flames dancing on the walls; there is a fire just out of sight deeper into the earth. You step inside, and soon you feel you have left the outside world far behind. The cave is narrow here, a path through the rock. You reach out to the cave walls and follow the path deeper inside, your fingers stroking the rough stone as you go. You notice there are patterns of ochre inscribing chevrons and sun wheels, and the sweeping shapes of animals running following the natural lines of the stone, strange and yet familiar. You know that generation upon generation of humans have walked this route before you. You can hear a slow gentle drumming, echoing from further in, like a heartbeat, and your footsteps take up its slow easy rhythm.

The path turns a corner, and you find yourself in a large cavern, with a huge central fire, burning brightly, its flames almost reaching the roof. All around are people; men and women of all ages, sitting on skins, their eyes glittering in the firelight. Some are performing tasks, weaving, sewing, whittling wood, but there is a feeling of relaxed ease about their activities. There is no rush. Others are eating, drinking, nursing babies, talking quietly. Several are sitting straight backed, staring into the flames, drumming together. As you look around, you see there are many animals in the cave also, and strange beings, which seem to slip in and out of focus as the light from the fire rises and falls. All these are your clan, your bloodline. Everyone here is peaceful and bonded by kinship.

Several people turn to look at you as you come closer, although none are alarmed. You make your way closer to the fire, and find a place to sit, and be.

This is the council fire of your ancestors, their hearth and heart fire. You will always have a place among them.

At some point you will be approached by someone, or something, and this will be your ancestral guide. They will know you, and although they may feel strange, even alien, there will be something comfortable about them, and their manner towards you, as if any unease is only on a surface level.

Spend some time with your ancestral ally. Get to know them and feel free to ask them questions. They may have things to share with you, and hold skills or power that is your legacy, and which you can receive now for your healing and blessing. They may alert you to the need for healing along your ancestral line. If so then they can be of assistance to you in making prayers or creating healing ceremonies so that your ancestors may be at peace, and any negative energy from the past is freed and transformed, making your life and those of future generations more positive as a result. They also may be of great reassurance, as they have walked this life before you, and are working with you because they have special understanding of the challenges you face.

Allow yourself to be very honest with your ancestral ally, very human. That way you can benefit the most from your contact. However, this is you first meeting with them, and you can call on them at any time.

You may also choose to ask the ancestral council for assistance. Here you may hear a whole range of responses, but this can be very powerful and illuminating. Your ancestral ally will act as a mediator so that you are not overwhelmed.

When it is time, or your ancestral ally suggests, give your thanks to your ancestors, and return the way you came, out of the cave, and through the forest and cross back through the door. Take your time before opening your eyes, and gently return to everyday consciousness. Begin by clenching and unclenching your hands, and wiggling your toes, before moving your body. Close down your sacred space when you are ready. Remember to ground yourself well afterwards, with eating and drinking. You may wish to record your experiences in a journal.

CHAPTER 5

Genius Loci and the Powers of Place

The primary source of power and relationship for the druid shaman must surely be the landscape within which we dwell. Our relationship to the land was once all powerful, and our ancestors depended upon it for all their needs. Now sadly that has become a thing of the past, and as our lives move more and more into towns and cities, and our food and shelter is supplied by others, often from far flung parts of the globe, it is easy to lose all touch with the earth beneath our feet. So often swathed in concrete and tarmac, it is easy to lose a sense of even the basic features of the landscape around us, hills and valleys, rivers and lakes. Sources of water become completely removed from our awareness, and are often forced along artificial lines. The curved hips of the earth around us are disguised by housing estates and high rises. But wherever you live, in the countryside, or in the city, the land remains, as does its host of spirits. Neglected and abused perhaps, ignored and forgotten; nonetheless, these must become our primary spirit allies, our firm friends and neighbours if we are to enter into any meaningful relations with the earth.

Our Celtic ancestors, and those before them, had a very different way of relating to the earth. There was very little chance of becoming a passive consumer of resources. The wild earth around them had a far more tangible presence, and was they knew, filled with gods and spirits of every kind. There were gods who transcended local cultures, and were revered by several or many tribes, even across Britain and Ireland and into Europe, but there were also local gods, the 'Genius loci' – spirits of place. These were the gods of the local rivers, hills, wells, mountains, who oversaw whole areas of the land. In addition there were also the other spirits, the in-dwelling spirits of trees, the wind and the rain, there were ancestors, spirits of the deep earth, the barrow dwellers, and of course there were also the faeries, the Sidhe. Spirits of every kind roam the earth, and our interaction and awareness of these beings, their effects upon the world, and ours, are the central work of the druid shaman. They were and are the universe in which we dwell.

Exercise 5: Gentle seer sight – seeing the energy and spirit presences of a landscape

To perform this exercise you will need to be sitting comfortably, somewhere where you can have a good view over the land, with your body in contact with the earth. A high place, or somewhere with a wide open expanse is perfect for this. In time with practise you will be able to experiment with other types of area.

Settle yourself comfortably, sitting with your back straight, take three deep slow breaths, and perform the tree posture (see exercise 1: the tree posture). With every out-breath, turn your attention to the earth beneath you, far into the soil and rock, to the earth's molten heart. Then slowly visualise that you have a tail, or roots, burrowing deep into the earth, and drawing up the heat, the energy of the earth's heart, up into your body. With every in-breath, see this energy rising higher and higher, filling your belly, your chest, into your arms and legs, and rising up your spine. Take your time. Eventually the energy rises up your neck into your head, and up across your brow and into your crown. Gently raise your arms as you sense this, to shoulder height, to hold the energy in your body. You may also draw in energy from above, if you wish, before lowering your arms again slowly, so as to be comfortable. Let your focus soften, feeling your attention dwell on this inner energy connection. Now look out across the landscape, with your vision softened. Try not to focus your eyes on any one thing, and keep your mind focused primarily on your deep steady breaths. Let your eyes half close, and your face relax.

In time you may see colours, or shimmering shapes as if you are looking through a heat haze. You may see things or even beings at the edges of your vision. Don't turn your head, but keep your back straight, and your face straight ahead. Take note of what you see, but don't adjust your vision. Just allow it all to *be*. Some of the things in the landscape around you may have subtle shifts in appearance, or be overlaid with other details or shimmers of colour. The world of spirit has an endless array of forms. Don't analyse what you see, at least not yet. Just open your awareness in a state of acceptance.

After a while you will feel yourself settling back into everyday awareness. Spend a moment visualising the energy you raised slowly descend back into the heart of the earth, and retract back into the sky. Let your tail or roots retract into your body. Take your time, and gently begin to move around. Stamp your feet to bring yourself back into your mortal everyday body.

You may need to ground yourself even more by eating and drinking. You may also want to record your experiences in a journal.

This exercise may need to be repeated several times in order to be successful. You are teaching yourself seership, and this is rarely done in a day, nor should it be. Be patient, and take your time, treating anything you see with open acceptance. You can analyse what you see at a later date, if you wish, but don't expect spirit to conform to your expectations, or logical thinking. The spirit world does not conform to psychological symbolism. It is itself. The spirits and energies of the land exist independently of you and your understanding. If you have a glimpse of them, open and expand your understanding of the world to accommodate them, do not shrink them down in your mind as the furnishings of your imagination. They will not care or even necessarily notice if you do, but you will be lesser for it.

Guardian spirits

Many landscapes will have an overarching spirit, or guardian. Sometimes these are plant or tree spirits, at other times they are faerie or ancestral beings, animal spirits, or the local gods themselves. Sometimes, especially at sacred sites, there may be several guardians, some of which served there during a mortal life, or made contracts to remain there after death. This is often the case at burial mounds, where such spirits may be ancestral councils, still available to advise us today.

The most powerful spirits of place are of course the local gods and goddesses, who were honoured by the tribes that once lived alongside them. Some of these over time become morphed together or associated with other more famous divinities. The evolution of their names and characteristics often mirror the movement of peoples and development of cultures. Yet still they remain. While sometimes their original names are forgotten, and they may prove hard to contact, their presence at their original site is never truly diminished, often being merely withdrawn slightly from human consciousness. Working with guides and other guardians related to a specific place on the earth is extremely helpful here, as they can gradually draw us into greater and greater communion and show us new, or even forgotten ancient ways of working which these greater spirits and deities recognise and are attracted by.

When developing a connection with a specific sacred site, or establishing contact with a local god or goddess, it is a good idea to try to meet and work with a general guardian spirit first. These can be similar to guides in as much as they can give useful information and mediate with other energies and beings for us, but they are also concerned with protecting and preserving the area and its energy. They are sometimes the primary being involved with working with the currents of life force, sometimes known as 'dragon' or 'ley' lines in an area. Guardians will sometimes want us to pass a test or undergo a form of initiation to work with them, or before they will introduce us to other beings or aspects of an area. This may sound ominous, and in ancient times, these tests and initiations may have been severe. Now, however, they are often more subtle, but treating a site or guardian with disrespect can still have many repercussions in our everyday lives, in our health and fortune. The best way forward with such contacts is honesty and respect. There is nothing wrong with explaining that much of the old ways and codes of conduct have been forgotten, and this can really help to effectively re-establish meaningful relations. Often, with patience, these initial approaches develop into a profound connection, and can result in attaining a powerful spirit ally, which will help access deep powers of the earth as well as the local divinities.

Exercise 6: Meeting the guardian spirit

This exercise can be performed in any outdoor space, but is especially useful in sacred sites. It can also be used to journey to a sacred site at a distance, so long as you know what it looks like in good detail. If you are performing this from a distance it will be more effective if you have visited the place physically, and even better if you have told the spirits there you will visit in this way. But it is still useful to enable you to visit a site you have never been to before, and is a good way to make an initial contact.

If you are looking to contact the guardian of a barrow, stone circle, or other enclosed space, begin your journey just outside the space, so you look ahead to it and enter in, where appropriate.

First, if you are doing this at home, you may wish to create your own sacred space, and/or cast a circle. Then sitting comfortably, take three slow deep breaths, and begin to draw energy up from the deep earth, using the tree posture (see exercise 1: the tree posture). Visualise yourself growing a tail or roots, which extends deep into the heart of the earth itself. With every out-breath, your roots go deeper and with every in-breath, draw the energy up into your body, like warm golden light. Gradually raise your arms, to hold the energy around your head, before gently lowering your arms again so as to be comfortable.

Next visualise before you two oak trees, with a simple path between them, leading to the sacred enclosure... Take a moment to stand at the threshold, and ask aloud that you may meet the guardian of this place, in kinship. Also ask any guides and allies that you have to accompany you.

Follow the path, and take your time to look around you. Are there any differences between the site in the mortal realm and here, seen in spirit? Ahead of you the site comes clearly into view, and a being stands at its entrance. They may be of any form. How do they appear to you? Approach them slowly and greet them respectfully. As you draw near, a gift for them may appear in your hands, which you may give to them.

Pay attention to their response, and to the behaviour of your guides and allies. Is it appropriate to continue? If not thank them and ask if you may come again. Wait a moment for their reply, and return along the path back between the oak trees and back to your body.

If it is OK to continue, you may ask the guardian some questions, and they may also question you. In time, see if you have permission to enter the enclosure. You may ask the guardian what sort of activities take place there. What was its original purpose? Has its purpose changed over time? What is the best way to work with this site? Are there rules and traditions to follow? How was it constructed?

A very important question is what can you do to serve and assist this sacred place... would it ask anything of you? What can you do for it?

Each interaction and communication with a guardian will be different, even for the same person, with the same spirit on different occasions. This is the first step in a long process, the first meeting of a long relationship.

When it is time, return along the path, through the oaks, back to your body. Take your time. First pay attention to the energy you raised from the earth, and see it return to the earth's heart, and gently retract your tail and roots. Then return another level to your body and everyday consciousness, by wiggling your toes and fingers first, before moving around. Close down your sacred space, and ground yourself carefully, perhaps with eating and drinking. You may also like to record your experiences in a journal.

Tree spirits

One common kind of guardian within a landscape is that of the tree or plant spirit. Far longer lived than many humans, the physical tree they inhabit, or one of its ancestors, may well have been specifically planted to watch over an area, and many sacred sites were primarily special trees in and of themselves. The druids have always fostered a close relationship with trees, and as embodiments of the great world tree, as well as wise allies of the green world, the druid shaman must develop this relationship not only with the practical magical and herbal aspects of different trees, but with their resident spirits as well. In Celtic lands many of the tree spirits have specific names, but today we may generically refer to them as dryads, which was the name of oak tree spirits in ancient Greece.

Exercise 7: Contacting a tree spirit

This can be done in one of two ways, firstly in the direct physical presence of a particular tree, and secondly, purely in 'vision'. If there is a particular tree in a landscape that you are drawn to, then work with that, and if it is not possible to be with it physically due to interruptions of some kind, then visit it, and spend some time in its physical presence for as long as possible, and then say out loud to it that you will visit it later in spirit.

45

If you do not have a particular tree in mind, decide on a type of tree – oak for example is a great one to try, but there may be another type that attracts you, and journey to meet its archetypal spirit.

First make yourself as comfortable as possible, creating a sacred space or casting a circle as you feel appropriate. If possible sit with your back against the tree trunk, as comfortably as you can, leaving you to concentrate on what you are doing. Next, calm and centre yourself with three deep breaths. Then raise your energy from the earth until your body is filled with light, slowly raising your arms into the tree posture (see exercise 1: the tree posture) before lowering them again. Remember to keep your back straight, and your breathing steady, deep and even. In your mind's eye, visualise yourself as connected to the energy you have raised from the earth by a long tap root extending deep into the ground, and with every breath, the energy rises up your body and lowers again. Then turn you attention to the tree trunk, and with every in-breath, feel the energy rising up your body, and the trunk of the tree, in unison, lowering together with every out-breath. Gently let your attention wander into the tree's roots, also extending deep into the ground, and your own roots with it and around it, as well as up into the branches. Take your time, then draw your attention back to the trunk.

Next extend your senses a little further, and ask that the spirit of the tree makes itself known to you. This may take any form, so be gentle and patient, and tune your senses into noticing subtle shifts. The spirit of the tree may give itself a humanoid form to make it easier for you, or it may not, and you must remember that this is a being quite different from yourself. It does not speak with words as a human, or have a human form, unless it utilises these things to aid communication. You must make similar effort and give similar respect to your connection, and accept the tree spirit as it is, without any projections as far as that is possible. Look for a sense of Presence, and slow, subtly shifting atmospheres, which may be the tree's natural form of communication.

If you feel welcome and able, ask the tree to show you some more of its being, ask what is it like to be a tree? Allow yourself plenty of time, and try to keep your perceptions clear, so that you may listen and feel the tree, and its communion with you.

Ask if you may connect with it again, and if it may help you to work with other trees and plants in future.

When you are ready, or if you feel the connection with the tree is starting to fade, thank the tree verbally for its connection, slowly open your eyes, and draw your attention back into your body. Visualise yourself drawing up you roots back into your body, and slowly wiggle your toes and feet, your fingers and your hands, to steady yourself back into your body before rising. Ground yourself afterwards with eating and drinking, and perhaps record your experiences in a journal.

This is a good exercise for first contact with a tree, and can be duplicated with the same tree on consecutive visits, where you will find that you naturally finesse the exercise and make subtle alterations to personalise it for you and the specific tree in question. It can also be a basic framework for working with plants, although sitting against them is not so easy, nonetheless, the pattern of their energy field and physical structure is broadly the same.

Nemetona and the nemeton

Nemetona, the Celtic Goddess of the sacred grove (or nemeton) was well known and her worship was once widespread across Celtic Europe, Britain and Ireland. However, Nemetona is likely to also have been the public name used for many local goddesses and gods, whose individual names were kept as powerful 'Mysteries', secrets known only to initiates. In Celtic Europe and Britain a nemeton was not only a sacred enclosure of trees, but took many forms; circles, henges, sacred wells, etc. Often a nemeton was a sacred complex which contained many features.

Nemetona is mentioned in inscriptions found in England and Germany, as well as being referred to by several Roman writers recording Celtic practices. We know that there were a great many 'nemetons' in France, Germany, Spain and England. The Irish lore refers to 'Nemed', husband to the Goddess Macha, as well as the 'fid-nemed', or sacred grove, which like Nemetona and nemeton spring from the proto-Celtic root word 'nemeto' meaning sacred space or sanctuary. The Romanised Nemetona is often referred to together with a male partner, often the God Mars, who in turn was often Celticised into a god of protection and agriculture. However, sometimes, Nemetona becomes masculine, and is morphed together with the male guardian deity, as in the inscription in Nettleham, near Lincoln, which refers to *Mars Rigonemetis* – 'Mars king of the sacred grove'.[6]

Nemetona may also, however, be associated with the Irish Battle Goddess Nemhain, and some nemetons may have been the site of grizzly practices. We know that many housed the heads of heroes and revered ancestors, often in special alcoves, as well as the heads of enemies which were often placed atop wooden spiked palisades.[7] We know from Roman writers at the time, that the heads of revered enemies were sometimes offered up to temples, and Tacitus writes of human sacrifices taking place in sacred groves on Anglesey.[8] Lucan refers to similar practices going on in Marseilles.[9] No matter how biased some of these accounts may be, there is archaeological evidence supporting the importance of heads and skulls at numerous Celtic sacred sites. The relevance of the head to the Celts is a vast subject, as the seat of power and spirit. However, for the druid shaman today, it is clearly best to approach these sites, and their guardians, slowly and respectfully, taking note that the culture we live in today is very different, and we must remain conscious of all we do; who and what we connect and commune with, and why.

Nemetona's ancient practice of both protecting sacred sites of all kinds, as well as facilitating human communion with them, continues to this day. Nemetona functions as divinity, guardian and guide to understanding and working with the powers of place in any given area, and contact with her (and/or him) is invaluable when working with a landscape or sacred site.

Of course we also know the names of many local goddesses and gods across Britain. There is the Goddess Tamara of the river Tamar, Coventina the Goddess of sacred springs near Coventry, Sulis, the Goddess of the hot springs in Bath, and Madron the Goddess who gave her name to Madron in Cornwall. We know of Mannanan the God of the Isle of Man and many more. But working with Nemetona, as well as guides, guardians and other mediators, can still be very worthwhile, especially in attracting the attention of deities and other beings that may have drifted far from humanity over the centuries, or in suggesting effective ways of working with them. In this way a balance can be discovered between re-initiating ancient traditions, practices and connections, and informing the development of new ones.

Ancestors and bloodlines

To the spirits of place, humans are short lived, fleeting beings, living on the surface of reality, middleworld dwellers. As individuals, our presence and effectiveness is limited. However, we were all once part of a long stream of ancestral presence in the landscape. Generation upon generation living and breathing upon the earth, drinking the waters from the same streams as our grandparents and their grandparents, eating food grown from the same soil, year after year, century after century. Hunting and eating and wearing the hides of the same herds generation after generation. Our blood and bone was literally made from the earth we walked upon, and returned to it one way or another upon our death. To the spirits of the land, then, we may be seen in terms of this long chain of being. Of course now we move around a lot more, and this complicates the issue, but still we are part of that ancestral chain, and that long tradition of human interaction with the land. If the spirits of place do not recognise us personally, they will recognise in us aspects of those who have gone before, for good or ill.

To deepen our connection with the land upon which we dwell, we need to make our minds and bodies resonate with its distinctive qualities. This can involve many things; simply spending time roaming and exploring the landscape, as well as sitting in quiet communion do much to open our eyes to the spirit of the land, and will attract their attention. Eating local seasonal produce will literally put the life force of the land itself into our systems, and cannot be overlooked as a vital way of strengthening our connection, as does drinking from a local water source, where possible. Another way of making connections with the spirits of the land is by making offerings.

There's a long tradition of giving offerings to the spirits of place in the Celtic lands. Domestic offerings were placed in storage pits, and larger ritual deposits in special ritual shafts. Offerings were also made to lakes and rivers, and beneath the post holes of buildings. There is much debate over whether these were propitiary in nature, to appease the gods, or served other purposes. However, it is likely these were a form of ritualised exchange, not based on keeping 'vengeful' gods happy out of fear, but rather a method of giving back to nature and to the spirits of place, out of desire for interchange and interaction.

Traditional Iron Age Celtic offerings were often rather grand – swords, coins, and jewellery, although offerings of 'Bog Butter' have also been discovered, a fatty substance like butter buried in bogs in Ireland and Scotland, some of which date back to the Bronze Age. We also know from the Roman writer Pliny that the Iron Age druids gave offerings of honey to the spirits of the earth when gathering vervain near the Summer Solstice, when the star Sirius was in the sky. Later Celtic offerings in the British Isles and Ireland are more domestic and agricultural, such as cakes, ale, cream, milk and grains. These were often deposited on special stones, known in Scotland as *'gruagach stanes'* or *'brownie stanes'* (stones), which have cup-shaped depressions. One such brownie stone, also known as the 'milking stone', is on the tiny Scottish Island of Hirta. This stone is of such importance to the local community that in 2012, after some geologists disturbed the stone, the National Trust for Scotland gave it an official offering of milk to appease the spirits.[10] Some of these stones may have a history of offerings going back to the Neolithic, though it would be difficult to prove in the case of biodegradable materials. However, many standing stones, stone circles and henges also received various offerings, which included human and animal skulls, pottery and unused stone axe heads and maces.

Another type of offering, still made today are known as 'clooties' – strips of ribbon or cloth hung on special or sacred trees, often those by holy springs. These cloths were once used by healers and cunning men; having been dipped into the waters with incantations spoken over them, they would be applied to the bodies of those in need, to receive healing from the spirits of place. They also take the form of prayer cloths, linking the person who has given the cloth to the spirits of the area. Sadly, however, this custom often gets abused and misunderstood nowadays, with sacred sites being littered with all sorts of strings, plastic wrappers and even bras and socks as clootie substitutes. Most of these do not biodegrade, and constrict both the tree's ability to grow and its access to light.

Offerings today should be thought about carefully. In today's consumer-led society, it is easy to think that anything we happen to have in our pocket, or something we have bought will work and be appropriate as an offering. However, the important feature must be the energy put into it – the care and time spent to make it – the thought really does count. Offerings today must always be biodegradable, that way, when the life-force of the gift has been consumed, the physical matter can return to the earth, or be eaten by local wildlife without harm.

We must also consider where we leave our offering. While in the past offerings were sometimes buried, this may not always be suitable now, especially at sacred sites which are often also sites of archaeological significance. We are trying to give to the land, not damage it. However, offerings buried in our own garden are another matter, and can help connect us to the land in a very literal way.

In general offerings of baked goods, homemade butter, honey or alcohol, such as ale or mead are good. If you have to buy something, it is possible to make prayers over it, to add some of your own energy. You can also make simple vessels of leaves, ivy wreaths, and moss to hold them, thus still putting some of your own effort into the gift.

One of the best gifts you can give to the powers of place is your care. Always have a bag to pick up rubbish, keep an eye on its wildlife and environmental quality, and get involved with local groups to ensure its welfare in a practical way.

Exercise 8: Offering ceremony

Try to make giving your offering a conscious act of intent, really reaching out to the spirits of place as you do so. One way to do this, is to get into a gentle meditative state, and really use your senses and awareness to decide first where you will make the offering. Perhaps there is a hollow in some tree roots, or a nicely placed stone or small enclosure that would be suitable. If your offering is food, consider if the local wildlife will be able to get to it, as well as whether it would be safe for them. Then try to tune in further still, and see if you can get a sense of the place's guardian spirit, if it has one. Finally, make your offering by placing it gently and reverently in position – don't throw or tip it – but give it with care and respect. Say aloud to the spirits of the place that this is an offering for them, that you give out of friendship alone, and ask that they receive it as such. You may be reaching out to beings you have no real sense of at this time, but they will notice you. Take that into consideration.

Finally, repeat your offering, both the type of gift, and the way and place it was given, often, every time you visit, month after month. In their own time, they will answer you.

CHAPTER 6

Climbing the Tree

The spirit realm and the Celtic Otherworld

We now turn our attention to deepening our explorations of the Otherworld, and familiarise ourselves with the terrain. Celtic Otherworldly cosmology varies across time and regions, but there is evidence from grave goods, especially food and drink found in Gaulish graves, that belief in an afterlife was strong. The soul was considered to exist and survive beyond death, hence the need for foodstuffs, feasting materials, weaponry and other riches for use beyond the grave.

In Wales and Ireland our knowledge of the Otherworld has retained more detail in folklore and mythology, as well as oral tales. Essentially this is a happy place, ageless and harmonious, full of feasting and enchantment, gods, magicians, faeries, talking animals and magical objects. Yet it is also a place where battles are fought between heroes, quests are won or lost, and lovers are enticed. When abused or disrespected, it also harbours monsters and horror for the arrogant or unwary, such as during King Arthur's disastrous raid upon the underworld, which features in the 10th century Welsh poem *Preiddeu Annwn* (The Spoils of Annwn).[11]

The Celtic Otherworld is a fluid destination, found as a group of disparate islands in the western seas, often discovered via *Immrama* or shamanic sea voyages, as a realm beneath the Atlantic, such as the land of sea god Mannanan Mac Lir, *Tir fo Thuinn* (land under wave) as well as in hollow hills, or *Sidhe*, the realm of the faeries or *Tuatha de Danann*. It can also be a feasting hall or hostel, known in the Irish as *'bruidhen'*, found in numerous tales such as that of High King Conaire Mor and Da Derga's Hostel, which is revealed as the land of the dead.[12]

The Otherworld may function as a land of the dead, but as the Irish word Sidhe may mean ancestor, faerie, or hollow hill, we find that these functions cross over and intermingle, and the peoples of the Otherworld and the land itself are sometimes indivisible. They can even at times subtly overlay the everyday world as well, especially at times when the 'veil' between the realms is thin, such as at the festivals of Samhain and Beltane (October 31st and May 1st respectively). The Otherworld's various destinations also contain widely differing activities and atmospheres. The house of Donn, or *'Tech Duinn'*, thought to be a rocky isle off the south-west coast of Ireland, was reserved especially for the dead, as the grave mound of the god Donn himself, who is associated especially with shipwrecks. Several other gods of the dead, such as Bile, were said to transport souls to his land. There is also *'Dun Scaith'*, the fortress of shields, or fortress of shadows, and *'Hy Falga'*, another name for the Isle of Man ruled by the faery King Midir.

We also find places of extreme beauty and festivity in the Otherworld. There are a great many in this category, such as *Tir na nOg* (the land of the ever young, or land of youth), *Tir Tairnigiri* (the land of promise), *Tir Na tSamhraidh* (the land of summer), *Tir Na mBeo* (the land of the living, or ever living), *Magh Mell* (the plain of happiness) and *Tir Na mBan* (the land of women).

These Otherworldly lands or islands are mostly found in the Irish and Manx traditions, but we also have the Welsh/British Otherworldly realms of *Annwn* (the underworld, or inner place, realm of ancestors) as well as *Gwynfed* (the upper world of the gods), *Abred*, or the spirit aspect of our mortal realm, and *Ceugant*, or infinity, as well as *Avalon*, which like many of the Otherworldly isles in the Irish lore is reached by travelling over water. All of these destinations also go under the title of the *Blessed* or *Fortunate Isles*.

Finally we have the Otherworldly cities of the High Irish

tradition, from where the Irish gods the Tuatha de Danann came. These are a little more unusual as they are attributed to the four directions *within* the Otherworld, Gorias found in the east, Finnias in the south, Murias in the west, and Falias in the north.

The world tree

All these destinations are beautifully illustrated using the imagery of the World Tree, with Otherworldly destinations positioned upon both the branches (as upper world realms) and the roots (underworld realms) as well as a whole host of places in between, our own mortal realm positioned upon the trunk, a causeway for interaction with both the worlds below and above. To the druids, trees were of central importance within their groves or nemetons, sometimes being substituted with a central pole, known as a 'craeb' or 'bile' accentuating the tree's role as a

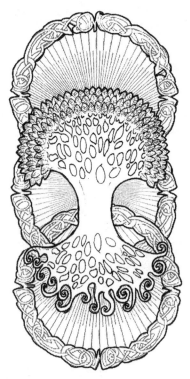

pivoting or axis point between the worlds. This world tree may have been, or envisioned as, a mighty oak tree, equal in depth and height, (although ash and yew trees were also of great importance in different areas). Taking their name from *dru*, or *duir*, as it is known in the Irish ogham alphabet, the importance of the oak tree to druidry is well known, functioning as both guardian and strong doorway – giving protection but also access to the Otherworld simultaneously – a primary guide and ally for the druid as shaman.

We will now explore the three worlds, as seen in the Welsh druidic lore, visiting each in turn, gaining allies in each in order to learn the skills we need and gain the insights we seek from each of the realms in turn.

The middleworld

The middleworld, known as *Abred* in the Welsh tradition, is our mortal, physical world. It is a place usually overlooked and disregarded as a spiritual resource, or as a home for beings other than the purely physical. Yet the mortal world abounds with spirits of every kind. Everything that comes to dwell in the mortal world has its indwelling spirit, whether tree, rock, river or animal. Weather fronts and oceans swarm with spirits, of wind and wave, of air and fire, in infinite configurations and diversity. Here we find 'elementals', the spirits of the elements, the local gods and powers of place, and the wandering dead. There are also animal spirits, the sidhe or faeries, and many other beings who defy description.

Relating to our land in a sacred manner is essential for any druid shaman. We must know our landscape intimately and lovingly, placing great care upon how we use its resources, and respond to its needs. We must be practical and proactive in protecting and restoring its wellbeing, but we must also acknowledge its indwelling spirits, as neighbours and kin, and good relations with them must be sought out and maintained at all costs. *'The good neighbours'* is an old name for faeries, and our folk tales and recorded oral history abounds with simple and sometimes powerful interactions with these beings. Simple gifts like bowls of cream and milk have often been given as offerings, and feature in our old lore sometimes as common everyday exchanges when the 'neighbours' appear, being different from the mortal inhabitants of an area and yet no more unusual than them. Offerings and gifts were also given to the sea, and the sea god Manannan mac Lir, to seek safe seafaring, and to the spirits of powerful natural features in the landscape, so that their indwelling spirits may help with healing, or the fertility of crops, for example. The importance of certain powerful sites, such as special trees and stones, was such that sometimes roads and building plans were altered lest the indwelling spirits were affected, and bad luck fall upon the perpetrators. Lack of consideration in the modern era for such factors has led to all sorts of problems, such as 'sick building syndrome' where the inhabitants grow ill or face misfortune for unknown reasons. Understanding and resolving such issues is very much the work of the druid shaman today.

One of the main ways to work shamanically with the middle-world, is to attain an animal ally. Animal spirits in particular can help with increasing our understanding of our physical, manifest condition. Although modern civilisation likes to believe we are very different from our animal cousins, we are in fact very similar, and our society works along very similar lines as the natural world, albeit in a symbolic, culturally constructed fashion. Animal allies therefore can help us become more present and inhabit our physical forms more effectively, and by extension become more effective as we interact with our environment, whether that be in nature, or in human society.

One key area of spirit interaction with the animal realm for humans is that of the hunt. Today, very few of us have a real need to hunt for food, yet its energetic ancestral pattern remains strong, and connecting with the hunter gods is still powerfully resonant for many – hunting as a source of food for others, as well as the metaphorical hunt – for meaning, for spiritual connection, and the quest for the soul, as well as culling and sacrifice - maintaining the balance, letting go of things no longer needed in order to bring in the new. Taking physical risks in order to provide for others was once an honourable thing, and remaining conscious of the life that is taken, as well as the life that is sustained as a result, is very much under the aegis of these gods.

The lord of the hunt or lord of the animals is a recurrent figure in the Celtic tradition. As both hunter and herdsman as well as prey, he is responsible for culls and sacrifice, as well as the earning of skill and honour. He has many names, Cernunnos, Herne, and in the Mabinogion he is the wild herdsman, *Custennin*, and the Black Giant. He is also Pan, among others, and these gods are as much 'the friend and helper'(as Kenneth Grahame put it in *The Wind in the Willows*) of the animal realm and the natural world, as they are the allies of our ancestral fathers in the distant past, facing down wild boar with only a spear in their hands. They are the mediators of life and death in the mortal world, with its ever rolling balance, just as much as their feminine counterparts, the goddesses who oversee both births and deaths in an ever re-balancing equilibrium. The hunter gods may also be understood as guardians of this ebb and flow, guardians of the Mysteries, and Otherworldly exchange and interchange, who must be encountered before deeper spiritual tuition and development may occur. As fatherly figures, these gods are responsible as guardians and providers for human needs, as well as protectors and spokesmen for the wild world... the realms of animals and landscapes untouched by human culture. They represent the wild spirit, the fierce, instinctual and experiential side of masculinity. As lovers of the Goddess in many of her forms, they are one half of the sacred dance that brings fertility to the land.

In order to attain an animal ally, and be granted access to the other worlds, we must first encounter the wild herdsman, the lord of the animals, and face his challenge.

Exercise 9: Finding your animal ally

First create your sacred space. Then, sitting comfortably, calm and centre yourself with three deep breaths. Then raise your energy from the earth until your body is filled with light, slowly raising your arms into the tree posture (see exercise 1: the tree posture). When you are ready, visualise an oak door ahead of you, and lower your arms so as to be comfortable. Remember to keep your back straight, and your breathing steady, deep and even. Focus on the door, and affirm to yourself your intention to visit the Wild Herdsman. This will clarify and set your destination. Next call your druid ally to you. This may be by calling them by name, or visualising an object or symbol associated with them. When you are ready, step through the door, and see ahead of you the path through the forest.

It is dusk, and the forest around you is full of life and noise. You hear rustlings, grunts, bird calls and strange unidentifiable sounds. The wind blows and rakes the leaves, and the trees creak and strain before falling silent. Ahead of you is a clearing, with a low rise of soft green turf, and a great oak tree in its centre. As soon as you break out of the tree cover, you feel the change in atmosphere. This is a sacred place, which seems to glow with a light that you cannot see but you can feel. It seems to emanate from the earth itself. You feel unseen eyes upon you from all around, and a great profound Presence. Ahead of you appears a large man, covered in shaggy furs, with a huge stag's hide wrapped about his shoulders. Antlers rise up from his head, and although you can see him clearly it is impossible to tell if the antlers are the stags, or rise from his own brow. Beneath he has dark, bright eyes that glitter and view you strangely, but not unkindly. There is an air of great power and animal scent around him, yet also the inescapable sense that here is something holy, sacred, beyond our knowing...

Take a moment and feel his Presence, looking into his deep eyes if you can. He may have messages or a gift for you. However, just communing with Him may be the most powerful gift of all. Allow yourself silence here.

Suddenly you see that by his side is a beautiful white hart, with magnificent antlers. Just as you take in the beauty of this creature, the Wild Man smacks it once, hard, on its head and it buckles to its knees, and collapses. At once, the stillness of the green mound is replaced by a great crowd of animals, of every kind, and the silence is broken by a great cacophony of calls and howls. The air is warm with their animal heat and breath. They press around you in the chaos.

One of these animals, however, stands before you, and appears in much greater focus than the others, as if despite the crowd, there is a connection of stillness and silence around you both and you stare into each other's eyes. The animal may be of any kind. Focus your intention on connecting and communing with this being. Move around each other, viewing the animal from all sides.

This is your animal ally. Do not allow confusion or doubt to steer you away from this knowledge. They may not be as you expected, but they have come to you here in this sacred place, in this ancient way. You may look around but the same animal will keep appearing until you accept them. They may challenge you, particularly the fiercer animals, the predators. If so you must stand up to them, and mirror their behaviour if that feels appropriate. This will be a sort of ritualised exchange, a formal greeting, and also forms your first great lesson from the animal realm and your ally. In whatever form it takes, spend time now with your ally, roaming around the clearing. You may go together into the forest, but remember your route and return to the clearing when you are ready. The Wild Man may have gone, but if you see Him, you must thank Him before bidding Him farewell. Your animal ally may then return with you through the forest from the clearing to the wooden door. When you are about to leave, ask them if there is a preferred way to reconnect again. This may take any form; just thinking of them, or using a name or visualising a symbol or object. Be open to their communication.

Often animal allies use body language or direct thought rather than words. They will not necessarily 'speak', but you will receive their communication if you take your time and are receptive to the form it takes. This will take practise but have patience. Once you have connected with them once, you will do so again and everything else will develop and finesse over time. If nothing else you will have a sense of their Presence, and the memory of this meeting. This will be enough to work with them again.

Thank your ally, and cross back through the door. Take your time before opening your eyes, and gently return to every day consciousness. Begin by clenching and unclenching your hands, and wiggling your toes, before moving your body. Close down your sacred space when you are ready. Remember to ground yourself well afterwards, with eating and drinking, and, if you wish, record your experiences in a journal.

Working with your animal ally

When you have attained and grown comfortable with your animal ally, you may begin to work with them in the outer middle world, our day-to-day realm. First you must make repeated visits to the great oak and spend time with them, before asking them to cross through the door with you, back to your sacred space.

When they have crossed through, take your time, and try to tune into their presence in the room with you. Allow your imagination to help you here, as an invaluable translation tool between physical matter and spirit. What do you think your ally is doing?

Is it walking around, sitting, climbing, sleeping? Make it an offering, either of food, or something physical like dance, or song, and ask it to share your experiences, to dance or sing with you perhaps. This forms a good pattern of exchange and interchange between you, and prepares the way for later work. You may find after a while your animal ally recedes from your consciousness, or you may ask it to leave you for a while, before inviting it to join you at another time.

On later occasions try asking it to join you for a walk or a short physical journey, and as you travel, tune in from time to time and check its behaviour and responses. It will have a great deal to teach you and can communicate a great deal about your environment, physically, energetically and even socially that you may not have been aware of. Developing a good relationship with animal allies takes time, but can have a powerful effect, as we begin to resonate with it, and can gradually adopt and adapt some of its attributes for our greater wellbeing and effectiveness. We also receive the benefits of walking through the world as well as the other worlds with its support and company – when you feel a good connection has been made, you can begin to take it with you on other shamanic journeys, as a primary guide and helper.

The underworld

The underworld is a place of roots, and buried treasure. It is a storehouse, and a place of profound power, where we can seek refreshment and renewal. If we imagine the world tree as a mighty oak, the underworld dwells beneath us, in the roots and the earth. Yet the tree extends as far down into the soil as it reaches above, to the same depth as the tree's height, the roots reach to the same width and spread as the branches. This tells us something important, that the underworld is essential, as significant as the central space – the trunk, and the branches above. The three realms exist in perfect balance, and so must we.

The underworld has been treated very unfairly in recent centuries, overlooked and disregarded, as a place of 'base matter', hidden unspeakable urges and horrors, akin to the monotheistic ideas of hell. It has been seen as a place of fear and torture. Yet this is not so. Our myths and legends, particularly in the writing of Taliesin and the Mabinogion, show us an underworld of beauty and wonder, with rich resources for the soul. A realm of ancestral presences, the underworld holds the memories of past generations and incarnations, that have descended like fallen leaves to make a rich fertile soil, within which we grow.

In the Welsh tradition there are two schools of thought as to the name of the underworld; *Annwn*, meaning the underworld, the 'in-world', or 'the very deep place'. This is an Otherworldly paradise, full of wise and magical creatures, an ancestral haven, mentioned in detail in the work of Taliesin and the Mabinogion. Another, drawn in part from the work of Iolo Morganwg, is to call the underworld *Ceugant*, roughly translated, this means 'infinity', and is considered to be the place of one-ness with God or Source. Morganwg was a devout Unitarian, and would be appalled at the pagan applications that have made his work famous today. To him, Annwn was instead a separate Otherworldly destination which was a place of fiery torment, a Welsh hell.

An interesting point which connects these two versions of the underworld, Annwn, and Ceugant, can be found in the poem attributed to Taliesin, called 'Preiddeu Annwn' (the spoils of Annwn) where we find at the heart of the underworld lies a precious cauldron...

Am I not a candidate for fame, if a song is heard?
In Caer Pedryvan, four its revolutions;
In the first word from the cauldron when spoken,
From the breath of nine maidens it was gently warmed.[13]

The cauldron is the most treasured possession within Annwn, and may be understood as a feminine receptive symbol, akin to the womb. Cauldrons in Celtic mythology are highly important, bestowing inspiration, food, and immortality, and culturally they bound families and communities together via communal feasting. As such they could be understood as representing the divine feminine, the life-giving Goddess. Here the cauldron/Goddess is accompanied by nine maidens, nine being a sacred number in the feminine mysteries. These women could thus be seen as priestesses, or aspects of the divine feminine Herself, who 'warm' the cauldron, igniting the matter within it. Within the cauldron we have a singular homogenous state, where all things are blended, and alchemically configured into new forms. Seen in this way, Annwn, and Ceugant – the one-ness of God, or Goddess, have similar qualities and functions, as both the grave and the cradle or womb and source of life. A similar cauldron may be that of the Irish god the Dagdha, known as the *'Undry'*, or 'cauldron of plenty', a gift from the Otherworldly city of Murias, which provided endless sustenance.

We may seek an underworld guide to help us negotiate this terrain. Often within the underworld, we encounter ancestral presences, the deep ancestors who lived long before we were born, as well as those journeying through after a relatively recent death. We may also encounter animals and other life forms that no longer walk the earth. We may find dragons, and giants, or titans, as well as beings who the Irish Celts call the Sidhe, or faeries. The name Sidhe deliberately has three meanings, that of faerie, and ancestor, showing how close we are to other forms of life and spirit – on one level we are all kin, children of the Goddess, born of the cauldron, as well as the third meaning as hollow hill or burial mound, often used as Otherworldly access points. When we find a good underworld guide, they form an essential mediator helping us connect with this place of transformations and the myriad of life forms we may find there. They help us convey and transmit knowledge and vital currents of energy from the deep earth, to the middleworld above.

When we explore the underworld, it may take many forms, but is not necessarily underground. Quite often it is a landscape with sky and every living feature you would expect above ground, but it has a distinct quality, a rootsy, deep feeling to it, that you must experience to know.

Exercise 10: Seeking an underworld guide

Begin by creating a sacred space, perhaps by casting a circle, and lighting a single candle in the centre. Sit comfortably, with your back straight. Take three deep breaths, and begin to raise energy from the deep earth, using the tree posture (see exercise 1: the tree posture). Visualise yourself growing roots, or a tail, out of the base of your spine, burrowing deeply and easily into the earth beneath you. With every out-breath see this tail going deeper and deeper, contacting the fiery heart of the earth herself, glowing with golden light. With every in-breath, gently stretch your spine, and begin to draw up this light, from the earth's heart, up into your body, filling your legs, your hips, your stomach. See this light filling your chest, rising up past your heart, into your head. Slowly raise your arms, to keep this energy around your crown, before lowering your arms gently. You need not draw in energy from above on this occasion.

Breathing slowly and deeply, first focus gently on the candle flame. See its flame as a slim column of light, reaching up above the room, beyond your sight. Also imagine this column of light descending below the floor, deep into the earth. It is accessing the underworld with ease, beyond your vision.

Now close your eyes and breathe slow, deep breaths. Visualise ahead of you an oak door, and affirm your intention to visit the underworld, and find an underworld guide. When you are ready, cross through the door. Now call to you any guides you already have. On either side of you are two oak trees. These are the guardians of your path. Ahead of you a track way leads off through a rich forest. The way is marked with a pale chalk path. Follow the path, taking note of anything you see along the way.

In time you approach a clearing, and within it, a huge oak tree. As you step into the open space, you feel the atmosphere change tangibly. This is a sacred, holy place. The oak, unbelievably huge, has a wide trunk, and its roots like massive serpents, twist and coil up above the ground and deep into the soil. Above, its branches tower up into the sky, impossibly high. The wind blows, and there is the sound of chimes and soft bells. You feel a great presence around you, but see no one. You are alone with your guides and allies.

Walk slowly around the trunk, reaching out your fingertips to touch its rough surface. What do you see? What do you feel? What are your guides doing? Ask aloud now that you may have access to the underworld and a guide to assist you.

You see below you a gap and hollow between the roots, a low earthen tunnel, made by a small animal. As you draw closer to it and focus upon it, it grows larger, until you are standing at the entrance of a cave, sloping off deep underground, the coils of tree roots are now gigantic, snaking along the walls, floor and roof.

Take your time, and slowly descend into the ground. The way is easy, although the momentum of your footsteps makes you go faster and faster, deeper and deeper.

Suddenly you come out into an open space. Before you is a being. They may take any form. This may be your underworld guide, or it may be a guardian figure, from whom you must receive permission to continue. Sometimes these beings are one and the same. Approach them respectfully, and they will take the lead in your communication. Ask if you may continue, and if they are your guide. If they are not, you may either return the way you came, or continue on the path, and your guide will appear to you later.

When you have found your guide, take your time with them, and feel free to ask them questions, especially about the best way for you to work with the underworld. You may also explore.

In time, you will feel or be told that your journey is coming to its conclusion. Thank your underworld guide, and return the way you came, along the path, and then ascending the tunnel quickly and easily. You climb back out of the tree roots, and through the forest, along the path and back between the two trees and the oak door, back to your body.

Bring yourself back into your body gently and slowly, wiggling your toes and fingers first. Then turn your attention to the energy you raised from the earth and gently return it, down into the ground, before retracting your tail and/or roots. Take your time before moving around, and when you are ready, close down your circle, or sacred space, and snuff out the candle.

If you feel you've been a long way and are finding it hard to feel 'back' try stamping your feet. Ground yourself further by eating and drinking. You may also want to record your experiences in a journal.

The upperworld

The upper world known as 'Gwynfed' or *'the white life'* in the Welsh Tradition, is the realm of the immortals, and can be understood as a place of perfect peace, containing the archetypes or blueprints of manifest reality. It is a source of inspiration, knowledge, and insight, the place where ideas are born. This is a place of gods and teachers, where we may find the very spark of creation within us originates. Myths of the upperworld abound, and a useful one to consider is Prometheus stealing fire from the gods… in many ways, we travel to the upperworld for much the same reason – to seek wisdom, vivification, inspiration, and ignite our lives with the breath of destiny, of the divine.

It is important to always consider the upperworld in balance with the underworld. Too much weight has been placed on the upperworld as a place of light. It has created a sense in monotheism, and the modern New Age, that the upperworld, the 'heavens' are somehow superior, morally and spiritually, compared to the middle or the underworld. This has created much damage, with a disregard for our earth, our bodies and those who see differently to us. Too much upper world has created intolerance, and arrogance, it has also created a babyish form of spirituality, where we expect beings from above to do all the work for us, to hand over responsibility for ourselves and our world, and trust they will make everything 'all right'. Instead we must remember to see all three worlds as a whole, a holistic system, each with their unique gifts.

We seek an upperworld guide, to assist us in remembering our soul's truth, our original purposes. We also seek a guide to the upperworld in order to access a worthy spiritual or magical teacher, to access divine knowledge, and to find inspiration about bringing new things to the world or our lives. Sometimes we seek the upperworld to bring renewal, a fresh start, a blank slate. As such it is always essential that we have worked in the middle realm, and the underworld first, that we have trans-formed and composted our 'stuff' and taken responsibility for our paths through life. That way, when we engage with the upperworld, we are not only suitably grounded, but can approach this realm as our own teachers first, as independent travellers, reclaiming our soul's destiny, not as spoiled children making demands in saccharine tones, or sobbing penitents, seeking forgiveness for our fallibility that we can only come to peace with within ourselves.

Exercise 11: Seeking an upperworld guide
Begin by creating a sacred space, perhaps by casting a circle, and lighting a single candle in the centre. Sit comfortably, with your back straight. Take three deep breaths, and begin to raise energy from the deep earth, using the tree posture (see exercise 1: the

tree posture). Visualise yourself growing roots, or a tail, out of the base of your spine, burrowing deeply and easily into the earth beneath you. With every out-breath see this tail going deeper and deeper, contacting the fiery heart of the earth herself, glowing with golden light. With every in-breath, gently stretch your spine, and begin to draw up this light, from the earth's heart, up into your body, filling your legs, your hips, your stomach. See this light filling your chest, rising up past your heart, into your head. Slowly raise your arms to keep this energy around your crown. Now turn your attention to above. Visualise a source of white starry light high above you, descending into your crown, and merging with the energy you have raised from below, until it finds balance in your chest, before lowering your arms gently.

Breathing slowly and deeply, now focus gently on the candle flame. See its flame as a slim column of light, reaching up above the room, beyond your sight; accessing the upperworld with ease, beyond your vision.

Close your eyes and breathe slow deep breaths. Visualise ahead of you an oak door, and affirm your intention to visit the upperworld, and find an upperworld guide. When you are ready, cross through the door. Now call to you any guides you already have. On either side of you are two oak trees. These are the guardians of your path. Ahead of you a track way leads off through the forest. The way is marked with the pale chalk path. Follow the path, taking note of anything you see along the way.

In time you approach a clearing, and within it, a huge oak tree. As you step into this open space, you feel the atmosphere change tangibly. This is a sacred, holy place. The oak, unbelievably huge, has a wide trunk, and its roots like massive serpents, twist and coil up above the ground and deep into the soil. Above, its branches tower up into the sky, impossibly high. The wind blows, and there is the sound of chimes and soft bells. You feel a great presence around you, but see no one. You are alone with your guides and allies.

Walk slowly around the trunk, reaching out your fingertips to touch its rough surface. What do you see? What do you feel? What are your guides doing? Ask aloud now that you may have access to the upperworld, and a guide to assist you.

Look up into the great branches. A soft light filters through to you, green and golden, touching your face. Suddenly you see a way up, via the rough bark of the trunk, and, hooking your arms into the lower limbs, you scrabble and pull yourself up.

The branches are huge, but you find your way higher and higher. When approaching the upperworld for the first time, or even the first few times, the ascent can be hard. Later journeys will be easier, and your upperworld guide may assist you, but here and now, you must put the effort in, and make the ascent through your own energy and will. Be persistent and keep at it. Up and up and up. Do not give in, it may seem the ascent is endless, but it is not.

Eventually the light gets brighter and brighter, whiter and whiter. Suddenly you break out at the canopy, the very top of the tree, and look out over a new landscape. You find you can jump out of the tree quite easily, and place your feet onto this new sacred earth. The land around you may be familiar, or quite unusual, but it will not be as you have seen it before. There is a feeling of freshness, and brightness, although it is not blinding, light seems to come from the very earth itself, from everything you see about you.

Before you a being stands. They may appear in any guise. This is your upperworld guide. Take your time with them, and feel free to ask them questions, especially about the best way for you to fulfil your purpose in coming to be born in the middle world at this time. You may also explore, or ask to have access to certain types of knowledge.

In time, you will feel or be told that your journey is coming to its conclusion. Thank your upperworld guide, and return the way you came, leaping easily into the top branches of the tree, and down into the forest, along the path and back between the two trees and the oak door, back to your body. The way back down is far easier.

Bring yourself back into your body gently and slowly, wiggling your toes and fingers first. Then turn your attention to the energy you raised from above, and see it retract back into the heavens. Then visualise the energy you drew up from the earth and gently return it also, down into the ground, before retracting your tail and/or roots. Take your time before moving around, and when you are ready, close down your circle, or sacred space, and snuff out the candle.

If you feel you've been a long way and are finding it hard to feel 'back' try stamping your feet. Ground yourself further by eating and drinking. You may also want to record your experiences in a journal.

CHAPTER 7

Seeking the Radiant Brow – Druid Shamanic Divination

The Awenyddion

There are certain persons in Cambria (Wales) called awenyddion or people inspired; when consulted about some doubtful event they roar out violently... and become as it were possessed by a spirit... They do not deliver the answer to what is required in a connected manner... but the person who skilfully observes them will find the desired explanation conveyed in some turn of a word: they are then roused from their ecstasy as from a deep sleep... These gifts are usually conferred upon them in dreams; some seem to have sweet milk or honey poured on their lips: others fancy that a written schedule is applied to their mouths and on waking they publicly declare that they have received this gift.

Giraldus Cambrensis, *Description of Wales*.[14]

This is a fascinating description of the Welsh *awenyddion*, literally 'one who is divinely inspired' from the 12th century, who functioned as a seer or soothsayer displaying striking similarities to those experiencing shamanic trances described in cultures all around the world. Note the suggestion that the awenyddion appears to be 'possessed by a spirit' and is in some state of 'ecstasy'... These are common features of shamanic practice, the close relationship between shaman and their spirit allies often appearing as a form of possession, although the balance of power between shaman and ally is far more equal than the term 'possession' suggests. Indeed often the term 'embodying' could be more appropriate. It is likely that figures like the one considered to be Cernunnos in the Gunderstrup cauldron wearing a deerskin and antlers were engaged in just this sort of practice.

Divination – to seek knowledge of the future or of hidden events – is a primary skill of the druid shaman. Whatever tool or focus is used, the shaman, druid or seer is seeking to understand the universe via the promptings of spirit; to read the pattern of 'the whole' to thus in turn be able to unpick one of the subtle threads between all things, and follow it to its conclusion, or next point of interchange, which reveals the knowledge or answer sought. While on the surface, it may appear that a single or series of questions is asked, in order to gain knowledge of spiritual, emotional or mundane events and relationships, beneath the surface, the spirit of the shaman/seer is in close dialogue with a whole host of other spirit intelligences, passing on the knowledge sought in a chain of communion and communication from Source, or the centre of the web. Often this is completely unconscious, and remains true whether the shaman seer uses card decks, pendulums, divining rods, or the ancient mantic practices of the Irish and Welsh shaman poets, the *filid* and *bards*.

To seek and receive knowledge from spirit, is to imbibe divine inspiration, to align oneself with a flow of interchange and exchange which stems directly from the gods, Great Spirit, or Source, however we view it. Celtic *bards*, or *filid*, while being keepers of genealogies and histories via the oral lore handed down through the generations, were also gifted seers; receiving this divine knowledge via a whole host of spiritual and magical practices. These were fundamentally shamanic in nature, the result of which would be the attainment of *glefiosa*, or the 'bright knowledge' – poetic illumination, where like Taliesin they would receive the 'radiant brow' of spirit vision – the knowledge of creation as a whole.

There are several techniques used by the filid, which remain very applicable today. These are *Tenm Laida, Dichetal do Chennaib,*

Imbas Forosnai, and the slightly lesser known *Neladoracht,* or cloud divination. Divination by fire and smoke were also used, as was meditation upon water, especially beside rivers and lakes. There was also the famous ogham alphabet, which was most likely a mnemonic system, for monument inscriptions, and was probably carved upon slips of wood, to cast as lots as a form of cleromancy, rather like Scandinavian runes.

Tenm Laida – Spirit songs

Tenm Laida or 'illumination of song' is the technique of shamanic spirit singing. Spirit songs are used in shamanic ceremonies all over the globe, and probably date back millennia; they are mentioned in several Celtic sources such as the Irish *Book of Leinster*[15] and featured in the tale 'The Death of Lomna'. Numerous Celtic tales refer to the hero Finn receiving divine inspiration by burning his thumb on the salmon of wisdom, which was cooking upon a fire, and ever after, whenever he chewed his thumb, knowledge would always come to him via a sudden song. This occurs after the death of his friend Lomna, in order that Finn can discover the identity of his corpse.

This technique was used right through to the modern era, with prayers and incantations sung in the Highlands being recorded in the *Carmina Gadelica* [16] as late as the early 20th century. Spirit songs can be used to invoke the spirits, bring healing and retrieve lost soul parts or power, as well as to seek divine knowledge.

Exercise 12: Spirit songs

First prepare your sacred space, and raise some energy using the tree posture (see exercise 1: the tree posture). Call upon your allies and guardians to assist you, and take nine deep breaths. When you are ready, begin your spirit song, by repeatedly chanting either *'Imbas',* (Irish: 'Inspiration') or *'Awen'* (Welsh: 'Inspiration'). Vary the tone and speed of your chanting, allowing yourself to improvise your rhythm. Then gradually alter the tones and pronunciation, to draw out the vowel sounds (I, A, E) and let the sounds you make shift and flow. Try not to think about what you are doing, but gradually step back consciously from what your voice is doing in order to share your song with your allies. Allow tune, rhythm and words to form or disintegrate of their own volition, as your voice becomes a channel for spirit.

You may choose to begin your chanting with a specific intention rather than with *Imbas* or *Awen*, by chanting 'healing come' or 'strength return' for example. Feel free to make up your own initial statement, and flow from there. This is very useful as a power retrieval exercise, as well as a form of offering.

Spirit will flow into your space and energy field via the power of your voice, and subtle shifts of consciousness will follow as a result. Allow the song to be the magic in and of itself, and if you choose to continue your ceremony with further work, let it remain 'of the moment' as a suitable precursor to later work, but significant and whole in itself.

Remember to close down your sacred space and ground yourself well afterwards, by eating and drinking.

Dichetal do Chennaib

Dichetal do Chennaib is notoriously difficult to translate. Commonly known as 'cracking open the nuts of wisdom' or 'incantation on the bones of the fingers' it may refer to the use of hand-ogham, by which the sections of the fingers all refer to specific trees and their cryptic poetic meanings. However, in the early Irish law tract, *Senchus Mor* it states that the fili/shaman could find out about a person, by placing their staff or wand upon the person's body. This was also used to find out about objects and who had touched them. This may be a form of psychometry, but is helped greatly by having a wand or staff that one works with closely, with the inhabiting tree spirit functioning as an ally, to assist in imparting the knowledge to you.

Exercise 13: Knowing by touch

First prepare your sacred space, and raise some energy using the tree posture (see exercise 1: the tree posture). Call upon your allies and guardians to assist you, and take nine deep breaths. When you are ready, slowly pass your hands, wand or staff through the energy field of the person you are seeking knowledge for – about 50cm from the body. If you are seeking knowledge from an object, hold it gently, or touch it with your fingers. Take your time, aiming for a gentle, non-focused meditative state where you may be able to receive the subtle messages coming to you. Allow your mind and eyes to relax. If you are working with a wand or staff, whisper to it, asking it to help you and thanking it for its assistance, then fall back into receptive silence. If you are just using your hands, focus your attention on the subtle feelings upon your skin, allowing your mind to quieten and your eyes to soften their focus. What are your first impressions? How does it feel to you right in this moment? Allow your allies, whether animal, ancestral, wand or staff – whatever form they may take – to guide and inform you subtly. Be open to their communication, before applying your analytical mind to the matter in any way.

Success for this technique is dependent upon having a close shamanic relationship with your tools, whether that be ogham sticks, wand or staff, or other equipment. Each of these tools will have their resident spirits which will assist you if you are suitably experienced. Success also depends upon a close relationship with your other allies and being fully present and receptive to what is being communicated. Therefore be patient and allow plenty of practise, and a good span of time before you expect any tangible results.

Imbas Forosnai

Imbas Forosnai, or 'knowledge/wisdom that illuminates', utilises the effects of sensory deprivation. Its description in the 10th Century *Cormac's Glossary*,[17] is possibly drawn from an even older and larger text the *Saltair Chaisil*. There are many instances in Celtic literature, where the seer or shaman retreats into a darkened hut or other structure for an extended period, to utter prophecy or magically poetic insights upon stepping finally out into the light. The description in *Cormac's Glossary* records that the *filid* (seer or shaman) first chewed upon pig flesh, an animal closely connected to shamanic or divine inspiration, or the flesh of a cat or dog, before leaving the meat as an offering to the spirits of place, the sidhe, or the gods. They then retreated into a darkened hut for the period of nine days, or until the wisdom and knowledge was received. This may be related to the *Tarbhfheis* or bull's hide ceremony which also utilised ritual food and trance-inducing darkness, in this instance by being covered by a bull's hide, in order to divine the next High King of Ireland. A similar technique may also be referred to in the Welsh tale 'The Dream of Rhonabwy'.[18]

Today we may not choose to spend so long in darkness, but we can utilise this technique, adapting it for our own needs and application.

Exercise 14: Seeking illumination

Give yourself plenty of time with this, at least an hour if not several hours. First prepare your sacred space, practically and energetically, closing all curtains and switching off all light sources other than one central candle. Place matches or a lighter next to the candle, and make sure the space is sensibly arranged so as to minimise any safety risks in the darkness. Raise some energy using the tree posture (see exercise 1: the tree posture), and make an offering to your gods or allies in whatever way you choose. A gift of food is most appropriate. Then settle into the centre of your space, suitably near your central candle, and snuff it out leaving you in darkness.

Take nine deep breaths, focusing your attention on your breathing before greeting the darkness itself and stating aloud your intention – to receive divine knowledge or the answer to a specific question. Then return your attention to slow deep breathing. In time you may choose to begin singing or chanting, may fall silent, or make other noises as you feel. This may well form a pattern of silence and song. Try not to get engrossed in any thought, letting your conscious mind slip over your thoughts without holding on to them. You may find images flash into your imagination, or you may have other sensory flashes. Allow them to come and go, to remember and analyse later.

Eventually you will feel it is time to light the candle. Do this as consciously and as deliberately as possible.

Initially this technique may take some extended practise to be really successful, but allow the feeling of new vision which arrives with the return of the light, to provide an insight into your question. The knowledge may come in a sudden insight, or a subtle shift of perspective. You may find the answer comes to you later, freed up by your stepping out of linear thought for a while.

Remember to close down your sacred space and ground yourself well by eating and drinking afterwards.

Neladoracht

Neladoracht, or cloud divination, relies on the key skills of gentle non-focused meditative awareness that are central to the other techniques. The Celts were fascinated by the winds and weather, believing that the sky illustrated and played out the Mysteries, life and death and the wisdom of creation being visible and spoken upon the sky.

Exercise 15: Cloud gazing

For this exercise you will need to go to a high place, preferably in nature, with an unrestricted view of the sky. Raise some energy using the tree posture (see exercise 1: the tree posture), and the sit or lie back comfortably in a position you can maintain for at least 30 minutes. Take nine deep slow breaths, and select a section of the sky you can see clearly without moving your head. This may be the whole horizon or a small section depending on your situation. You may at this point choose to ask a question of the air spirits, whether an open request for general insight or a particular matter.

Relax your vision and view the sky in a detached, meditative way, allowing the movement of the clouds, the flight of birds or anything else that goes by your vision to speak to you. Let any analytical thoughts pass by. Instead, in a relaxed way, try to read the sky as the body language of the air spirits, and of the universe itself. Keep yourself in a gentle, relaxed and receptive state, to feel what is being conveyed to you as the soul of the world speaking directly to your soul.

This takes practise, and what is received will often go beyond words. That is as it should be, as we are seeking profound spiritual connection more than literal mundane conversation. However, with practise, sometimes the messages will become particularly clear, in which case you should heed them very seriously indeed, as spirit has made extra effort to convey them to you.

Fire and smoke divination

Fire and smoke divination works in much the same way as cloud divination. We know that the druids preferred fires of rowan to warn and advise them prior to battle, and this is a very good wood to work with today. Try lighting a bonfire or hearth fire, and ask the spirits of the fire to advise you, adding slips of rowan if you have any, thanking the tree spirits for their sacrifice.

Relax your vision, and view the smoke and flame as you would the clouds, as a form of body language and expressive movement that goes beyond words and analytical thought. Fire and smoke divination is one of the easier forms to have success with, as our relationship with fire has been so close for so much of our evolution, and is very enjoyable. Take your time, practise, and greater levels of communication will come over time.

Conclusion

The pages in this book contain many doorways, each opening upon a spirit road which may lead us to a whole host of destinations. Gods, ancestors, and talking beasts have become our guides and friends. The druid shaman is a meeting point for all these beings and more, and can with practise become a capable Otherworldly traveller. Yet there is a challenge here, and choices to be made. Much of our Celtic literature is rich in lessons and resources, and together with history and archaeology we may learn a great deal about the druid shamans of the past, and may reconstruct large swathes of their practice. Yet in addition to this, and far more crucial, is the necessity to position this practice in the modern world. The Iron Age Celts and their druids, whether shamans, healers, priests or politicians, may be found around our ancestral council fires, but we are the ones who walk this earth today. Tradition and knowledge, while immensely valuable, are there to support our relations with spirit, not to replace them. The Otherworld is as accessible to us today as it ever was, and in opening ourselves to the numinous we may discover that perennial ecstatic wisdom that transcends and outlasts anything we glean from the past. The druid shaman's primary source remains: to be fully present in the here and now, with feet placed firmly upon our sacred earth. It is here that we find our power, and the hosts of the Otherworld waiting to greet us. The distractions of the mortal world may sometimes lead us away from this awareness, yet still the gods and spirits remain but a hair's breadth away, waiting for us to take a single sip from Ceridwen's cauldron and walk the shining paths with them, or have our souls set sail in their company upon the grey western seas.

Endnotes and References

1. Skene W.F. (Trans 1868) *The Four Ancient Books of Wales. The Book of Taliesin VIII.*
2. Cunliffe B. *The Celts – A Very Short Introduction.* Oxford University Press. 2003.
3. Carmichael A. *Carmina Gadelica.* Lindisfarne Press.1992.
4. Caesar. *De Bello Gallico VI 13-14.*
5. Matthew J. *The Celtic Shaman.* 2001. p43.
6. Green M. *Dictionary of Celtic Myth and Legend.* 1997.
7. Ibid.
8. Tacitus. *Annals XIV, 30.*
9. Lucan. *Pharsalia III, 399-452.*
10. Rangers diary (2012) *Good luck returns!* http://www.kilda.org.uk/blog/entry.aspx?ID=9bd70a24-ca2c-45f4-a0ad-69c91e58d6fa#.UQGgc7-vE_m
11. Skene W.F. (Trans 1868) *The Four Ancient Books of Wales. The Book of Taliesin XXX.*
12. Stokes W. (Trans 1902) *The Destruction of Da Derga's Hostel.* Reprinted from revue Celtique 22. Paris 1902.
13. Skene W.F. (Trans1868) *The Four Ancient Books of Wales. The Book of Taliesin VIII.*
14. Giraldus Cambrensis, from his *Description of Wales.* Ed. E. Rhys. pg 179. J.M. Dent and Co. London.
15. *Lebar na Núachongbála, The Book of Leinster.* Ed: R. I. Best and M. A. O'Brien. Dublin: Dublin Institute for Advanced Studies. 1967.
16. Carmichael A. *Carmina Gadelica.* Lindisfarne Press. 1992.
17. O'Donovan, John. (Trans 1868) *Cormac's Glossary.* The Irish Archaeological and Celtic Society.
18. Guest, Lady Charlotte. (Trans) *The Mabinogion.* London. 1877.

MOON
BOOKS

Moon Books invites you to begin or deepen your encounter with
Paganism, in all its rich, creative, flourishing forms.